corating

the
apple
press

A QUINTET BOOK

Published by Apple Press Ltd
293 Gray's Inn Road
London WC1X 8QF

ISBN 1 85076 009 8

This book was designed and produced by
Quintet Publishing Limited
32 Kingly Court, London W1

Art Design Bridgewater Associates
Illustrator Lorraine Harrison
Photographer John Heseltine
Editor Jean Elgie

Typeset by Context Typesetting, Brighton
Colour Origination in Hong Kong by
Hong Kong Graphic Arts Limited
Printed in Hong Kong by Leefung-Asco
Printers Limited

Cake Decorating

Contents

Basic icing requires little in the way of special equipment and you probably have most of the essential utensils. It is only when you have mastered the basic techniques that you need consider purchasing some of the more specialized items shown on the following pages.

Recipes for Victoria sandwich, whisked sponge and rich fruit cakes are given as these form a useful repertoire for cake decoration.

Equipment & Basic Recipes

BASIC EQUIPMENT

Wooden rolling pin

Spatula (plastic or rubber)

Wooden cocktail sticks or toothpicks

Measuring jug

Pastry brush

Sieve – 15 cm / 6 in size is the most useful

A selection of wooden and metal spoons

A selection of mixing bowls, preferably glass or china

String

BASIC EQUIPMENT

Hand-held electric mixer

Balloon whisk

Skewer

Palette knives –
13 cm / 5 in and 18 cm / 7 in
are the two most useful sizes

A set of measuring spoons

A selection of kitchen papers, which
should include greaseproof or waxed
paper, non-stick paper, cling film and
aluminium foil

Kitchen scissors. A smaller pair is
also useful for more intricate cutting

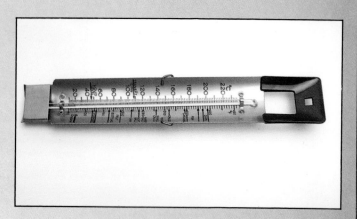

Most of the equipment mentioned in this section is available from good kitchenware shops and no doubt you will spend time browsing round and building up a stock. If you do not have a suitable store in your area, turn to page 128 for a list of mail order suppliers.

Sugar thermometer
This is essential for making some icings and frostings. Always check the temperature in boiling water before use.

Icing rulers and combs
These are usually made from plastic or metal. An icing ruler has one or two straight edges and is used to smooth royal icing across the top of a cake to give a good finish. An icing comb has one or more serrated edges, which may be pulled across some icings to give a 'combed' effect. A straight-edged icing comb is used to smooth the sides of an iced cake.

Icing nozzles
There are numerous nozzles available, but a basic requirement includes one or two plain writing nozzles, a selection of star nozzles and, perhaps, shell, leaf, basket and petal nozzles.

Metal nozzles are preferable to plastic ones as they give better definition. They are sold by numbers, but not all manufacturers use the same system of numbering, so always check on a chart before buying individual nozzles.

Look at the nozzles carefully before buying them. They should have no dents, the tips should be well shaped and the seams at the side should be well joined. Check that the points on a star nozzle are even. See pages 16–17 for more information on nozzles.

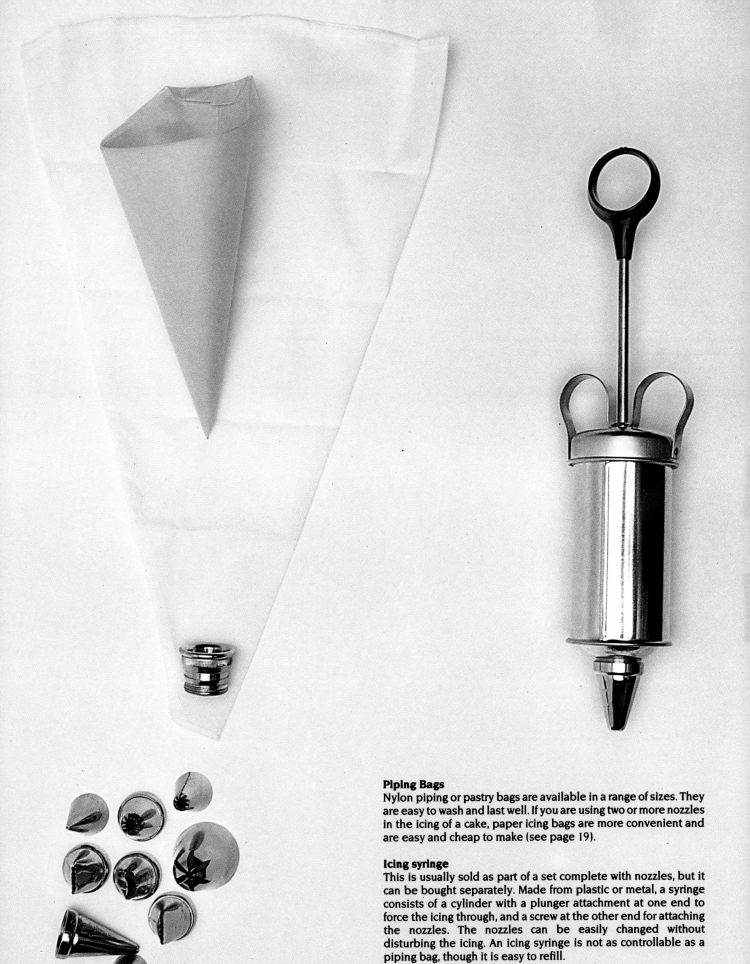

Piping Bags
Nylon piping or pastry bags are available in a range of sizes. They are easy to wash and last well. If you are using two or more nozzles in the icing of a cake, paper icing bags are more convenient and are easy and cheap to make (see page 19).

Icing syringe
This is usually sold as part of a set complete with nozzles, but it can be bought separately. Made from plastic or metal, a syringe consists of a cylinder with a plunger attachment at one end to force the icing through, and a screw at the other end for attaching the nozzles. The nozzles can be easily changed without disturbing the icing. An icing syringe is not as controllable as a piping bag, though it is easy to refill.

Turntable
Though not essential, if you intend to do a lot of cake decorating, a turntable is extremely useful. The cake is placed on its board on the turntable, which revolves as required so that you can obtain a good finish to flat icing the sides.

Cake boards
These are available in a number of shapes and sizes, usually about 1 cm / ½ in thick. They are covered in silver or gold paper and are useful to stand formal cakes on. Thin card bases are also available. Polystyrene cake bases can be obtained from some cake decorating suppliers and are excellent for practising flat or piped icing.

Icing nails and moulds
Available in a variety of different shapes, icing nails and moulds are made of plastic or metal with a metal stem. Nails are used as a rotatable base on which to ice flowers. A substitute can be made by pushing a cork on to the end of a skewer. Royal icing is piped on to lightly oiled icing moulds to make decorative shapes.

Cake markers and templates
Various rings and shapes are available in metal and plastic to help you to divide up a cake when designing a decoration. It is important that the design is even or it will look messy when finished. A pair of compasses will do equally as well.

Tweezers
Invaluable for positioning small decorations.

Paintbrush
Very useful for adding coloured details to run-outs and moulded shapes.

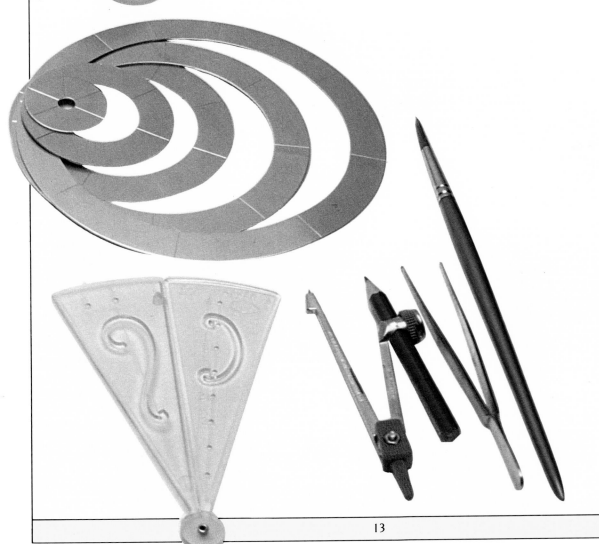

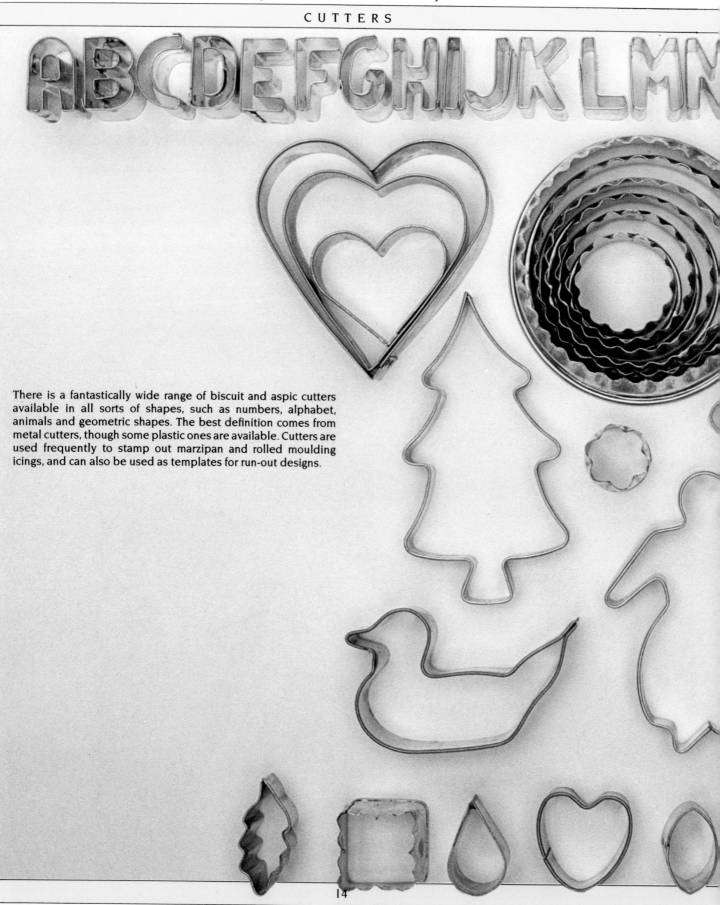

There is a fantastically wide range of biscuit and aspic cutters available in all sorts of shapes, such as numbers, alphabet, animals and geometric shapes. The best definition comes from metal cutters, though some plastic ones are available. Cutters are used frequently to stamp out marzipan and rolled moulding icings, and can also be used as templates for run-out designs.

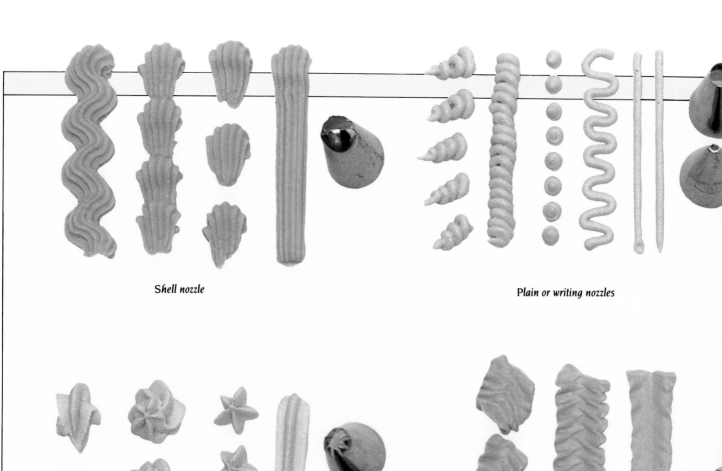

Shell nozzle

Plain or writing nozzles

Star nozzles

Leaf nozzle

Ribbon or basket nozzle

Petal nozzle

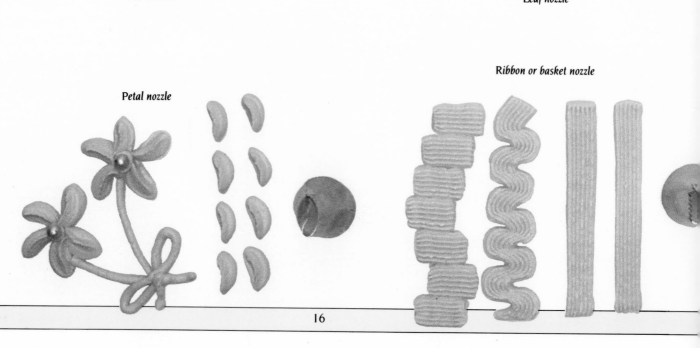

With just a few basic nozzles, you can achieve a wide variety of piped designs, as can be seen here. Though these are shown in butter cream icing, the technique of piping is the same whatever icing you are using. For more detailed instructions on piping designs in royal icing, see pages 82–87.

Large star nozzle

Large plain or writing nozzle

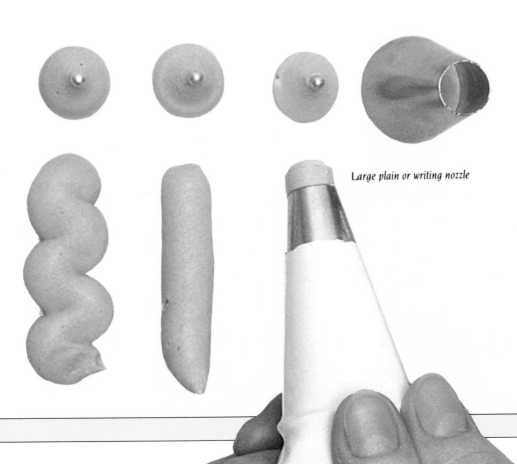

Small paper piping bags are invaluable for piping decorations with royal, glacé or butter cream icings as they are easier to control than larger piping bags or icing syringes. They are simple to make and take any of the small icing nozzles. Make up a batch of 10 at a time as you will probably use several for one cake and they can simply be discarded after use.

To make a piping bag

1 Cut a 25 cm / 10 in square of greaseproof or waxed paper. Fold it in half diagonally to make a triangle.
2 With the top point of the triangle facing towards you, roll in one of the side points to meet the top point.
3 Roll the other side point over the first one and bring round to the back of the top point.
4 Secure either by folding over top edges several times or by stapling them together.

To fill a piping bag

5 Snip off the tip of the piping bag and insert the required nozzle. Spoon some icing into the base of the bag. Fill to one-half to two-thirds full. Take care not to overfill as the icing will overflow from the top or the bag will burst.
6 Fold the sides of the bag in towards the centre, then fold over the top, pushing the icing down gently towards the tip. With care, the bag may be opened and refilled once or twice before being discarded.

You will inevitably discover the most comfortable position to hold the piping bag, but, basically, it should be held in both hands with the fingers at the sides, pressing down with the thumbs on the folded top part of the bag to squeeze out the icing. Pressing and releasing the thumbs will cause the icing to flow, then stop. Watch carefully all the time to see how the icing is flowing and you will quickly learn to judge the pressure and movement required to produce even, well-formed lines and shapes.

Insert a plain or writing nozzle and practise piping straight lines. Once you have mastered these, try using a star nozzle for rosettes, shells and scrolls.

All cake tins should be greased and lined (for non-stick tins, following manufacturer's instructions). For most light sponge mixtures, it is only necessary to line the base of the tin with a single thickness of paper. Use greaseproof or waxed paper, or a non-stick paper, which does not need greasing.

Lightly grease the tin with oil, melted butter, margarine or lard. Cut a piece of paper to fit exactly in the base of the tin and place it in position. Lightly brush the paper with oil or melted fat. If wished, the sides of the tin can be sprinkled with a small amount of flour, or a mixture of equal quantities of flour and caster sugar.

Always tip out any excess flour before spooning in the cake mixture.

The richer the cake mixture, the more likely it is to stick to the tin. For this reason it is better to line both the base and sides of the cake tin with a double thickness of greaseproof or waxed paper if you are making a rich fruit cake. For the larger size tins, which will be in the oven for about 3–4 hours, it is also a good idea to tie several thicknesses of brown paper or newspaper around the outside of the tin. This reduces the chances of overcooking the edges.

Base lining a round or square tin

1 Place the tin on a single thickness of paper. Draw round the base and cut out. Lightly grease the base and sides of the tin. Place the paper in position, then grease the paper with more oil or melted fat.

To line a round or square tin

For rich cake mixtures use a double thickness of paper; lighter fruit mixtures will require only one thickness of paper.
1 Cut a circle or square of paper to fit the base of the tin.
2 Cut one or two strips of paper about 1–2 cm / ½–¾ in wider than the depth of the tin and long enough to fit round the sides of the tin plus a little extra for overlapping at the joins.
3 Make a fold along one long edge of strips, about 1–2 cm / ½–¾ in deep, and cut diagonal slashes from the edge to the fold.
  Lightly grease the base and sides of the tin.
4 With slashed edges down, arrange the strips of paper round the inside of the tin (pressing well into the corners of a square tin). Lightly grease the paper.
  Place the circle or square of paper in the base to cover the slashed edges and grease lightly.

To line a Swiss (jelly) roll or other shallow rectangular tin

5 Place the tin centrally on a piece of paper about 4 cm / 1½ in larger all round than the top edge of the tin. Make a diagonal cut from each corner of the paper to each corner of the tin.
6 Lightly grease the tin and place the paper in position, overlapping it at the corners for a neat fit. Lightly grease the paper once more.

VICTORIA SANDWICH CAKE

Basic Victoria sandwich and one-stage mixtures chart

Egg quantity and tin size	Oven temperature	Approx. cooking time
2-egg quantity is sufficient for:		
2 × 18 cm / 7 in sandwich tins	180°C / 350°F / Gas 4	20 minutes
20 paper cases	180°C / 350°F / Gas 4	15–20 minutes
1 × 20 cm / 8 in (900 ml / 1½ pt) ring tin	170°C / 325°F / Gas 3	30–35 minutes
450 g / 1 lb loaf tin	170°C / 325°F / Gas 3	35–40 minutes
900 ml / 1½ pt pudding bowl	170°C / 325°F / Gas 3	50 minutes
1 × 15 cm / 6 in round tin	170°C / 325°F / Gas 3	40 minutes
3-egg quantity is sufficient for:		
2 × 20 cm / 8 in sandwich tin	180°C / 350°F / Gas 4	20–25 minutes
30 paper cases	180°C / 350°F / Gas 4	15–20 minutes
1 × 18 cm / 7 in round tin	170°C / 325°F / Gas 3	55 minutes
1 × 28 × 18 cm / 11 × 7 in slab tin	170°C / 325°F / Gas 3	35–40 minutes
1 × 900 g / 2 lb loaf tin	170°C / 325°F / Gas 3	50–55 minutes
1 × 23 cm / 9 in (1.5 litres / 2½ pt) ring tin	170°C / 325°F / Gas 3	40–45 minutes

To give a finished cake with a depth of approximately 5 cm / 2 in use:

Egg quantity	Tin size	Oven temperature	Approx. cooking time
2	15 cm / 6 in round	170°C / 325°F / Gas 3	40 minutes
3	18 cm / 7 in round 15 cm / 6 in square	170°C / 325°F / Gas 3	55 minutes
4	20 cm / 8 in round 18 cm / 7 in square	170°C / 325°F / Gas 3	1 hour
5	23 cm / 9 in round 20 cm / 8 in square	170°C / 325°F / Gas 3	1¼ hours
6	25 cm / 10 in round 23 cm / 9 in square	170°C / 325°F / Gas 3	1¼ hours
8 plus extra 1 cup / 100 g / 4 oz flour	28 cm / 11 in round 25 cm / 10 in square	170°C / 325°F / Gas 3	1½ hours
10 plus extra 1¼ cups / 150 g / 5 oz flour	30 cm / 12 in round 28 cm / 11 in square	170°C / 325°F / Gas 3	1½–1⅔ hours

This is a fairly firm, yet moist cake. it can be left plain or flavoured in many ways, such as adding grated lemon or orange rind, coffee or cocoa powder. Chopped nuts or glacé fruits and various sweet spices can also be added. You can experiment to find your favourites, although there is a list of variations at the end of the basic recipe.

A Victoria sandwich is often sandwiched together with jam, but it can also be iced with glacé icing, butter cream or frosting.

The basic Victoria sandwich mixture is very useful for larger cakes as it keeps well for several days in an airtight container. It freezes well, too. There are many shapes to bake the mixture in, so follow the chart as an easy guide to quantities and cooking times.

Basic recipe (known as a 3-egg quantity)

¾ cup / 175 g / 6 oz butter or margarine, softened
1 cup − 2 tbsp / 175 g / 6 oz caster sugar
3 eggs, beaten
1½ cups / 175 g / 6 oz self-raising flour
milk

Cream the butter and sugar together until light and fluffy. The mixture should drop easily from the spoon or whisk if tapped against the side of the bowl.

Add the beaten egg a little at a time, beating well between each addition, so that the egg is absorbed into the mixture.

Sift the flour and fold into the mixture. Add a little milk to give a dropping consistency.

Spoon the mixture into the prepared tins. Level the surface, then make a slight dip in the centre. Bake in a preheated oven (see chart) until cakes are well risen, golden and firm to the touch.

Allow the cakes to cool slightly in the tins, then transfer to a wire tray. Invert the tins over the cakes and leave until completely cold. This helps to keep the cakes moist while cooling.

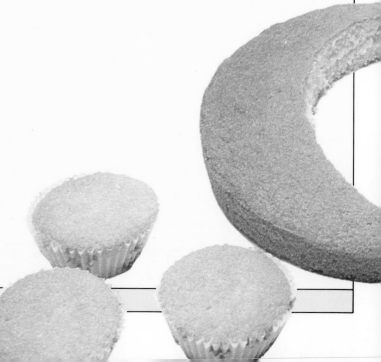

Variations

CHOCOLATE. Replace 1 tbsp flour with 1 tbsp cocoa powder for each 1-egg quantity.

COFFEE. Add 1 tsp instant coffee powder for each 1-egg quantity. If using coffee granules dissolve them first in a little hot water.

LEMON OR ORANGE. Omit milk. Add 1 tsp grated rind for each 1-egg quantity, plus a little juice to mix to a dropping consistency.

NUT. Add 50–75 g / 2–3 oz / ½–¾ cup chopped nuts to the basic mixture.

DRIED OR GLACE FRUITS. Add 50–75 g / 2–3 oz / ⅓–½ cup sultanas, chopped glacé cherries or chopped crystallized ginger to the basic mixture.

CHOCOLATE CHIP. Add 50 g / 2 oz / ⅓ cup chocolate dots or chips to the basic mixture.

COLOURED. Pink, green or yellow food colouring may be added to the mixture. Add several drops, as required. A marbled effect can be achieved by spooning alternate coloured mixtures into a cake tin, then swirling them lightly with a skewer.

One-stage mixture

This uses basically the same ingredients as the Victoria sandwich and in the same proportions. The main difference is that soft tub margarine is used instead of butter or block margarine. This means that the creaming stage of the butter and sugar is unnecessary, but extra raising agent must be added to compensate for this. Allow 1 tsp baking powder for every 3-egg quantity or for 2-egg quantity use ½ tsp.

As the cakes become larger, a little extra flour is required to hold the shape of the cake during cooking.

Basic recipe
¾ cup / 175 g / 6 oz soft tub margarine
1 cup − 2 tbsp cup / 175 g / 6 oz caster sugar
3 eggs
1½ cups / 175 g / 6 oz self-raising flour
1 tsp baking powder

Place all the ingredients in a bowl and beat well for 1–2 minutes while evenly mixed.

Spoon into the prepared tin, level the surface and bake in a preheated oven (see chart).

Variation

LEMON OR ORANGE. Add grated rind of 1 lemon and 1 tbsp juice. See also the variations for Victoria sandwich.

This is a very light sponge cake made by whisking eggs and caster sugar in a bowl over hot water. Once this mixture turns to a pale thick foam, sifted plain flour is very carefully folded in. No extra fat is added, so once baked this mixture does not keep well and is best eaten on the day of making, or the following day.

Basic recipe
3 large eggs
½ cup − 1 tbsp / 75 g / 3 oz caster sugar
¾ cup all-purpose / 75 g / 3 oz plain flour

Put the eggs and sugar in a bowl over a pan of simmering water.

Using a hand-held electric mixer, whisk the eggs and sugar for 5 minutes until pale and foamy. Remove from the heat and continue whisking for a further 3–4 minutes until the mixture is thick enough to form a trail.

Sift the flour, then fold into the egg mixture a little at a time, until evenly dispersed.

Pour into the prepared tins and bake according to the chart. The cake is cooked when it has just started to shrink away from the sides of the tin and springs back when pressed lightly with a finger.

Cool slightly, then turn out onto a wire rack. Invert the tins over the cakes and leave until completely cold. This helps to keep the cakes moist.

Swiss (jelly) roll

A Swiss roll is made with the basic whisked sponge mixture, but baked in a tin that measures 34 × 24 cm / 13½ × 9½ in. Line the tin with greaseproof or waxed paper that extends about 2.5 cm / 1 in above the edge all the way round.

Preheat the oven to 220°C / 425°F / Gas 7 and bake for 7–8 minutes until risen and springy to the touch.

While the cake is baking, lay a clean, damp tea towel on the work surface, cover with a large sheet of greaseproof or waxed paper and sprinkle liberally with caster sugar.

Invert the cake on to the sugared paper. Quickly peel off the lining paper and trim the edges of the cake. Make an indentation with the back of a long-bladed knife across one of the short edges. Use this to start rolling the cake, ensuring the greaseproof or waxed paper is in between each rolling of cake, and using the tea towel as an aid to rolling.

Wrap the Swiss roll in the tea towel and cool on a wire rack until cold.

When cold unwrap the roll carefully and spread with whipped fresh cream, butter cream or jam. Roll up again and dust with caster sugar. If using only jam as a filling, this may be spread on while the cake is still warm and then rolled up.

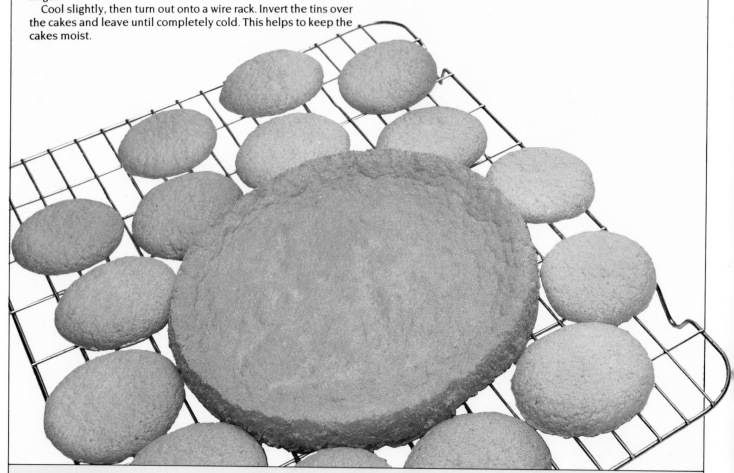

Variations

CHOCOLATE. For each 2 egg-quantity replace 15 g / ½ oz / 2 tbsp flour with 15 g / ½ oz / 1½ tbsp cocoa powder.

COFFEE. Add 2 tsp instant coffee powder with each 2 egg-quantity used.

LEMON OR ORANGE. Add the grated rind of a lemon or an orange with the sugar.

This chart is designed as an easy guide to show you how much cake mixture is required for various tin sizes.

The basic quantity of mixture is known as a 3-egg quantity, and is easily divisible. For example, for each egg you use 25 g / 1 oz caster sugar (1 tbsp sugar) and 25 g / 1 oz plain flour (4 tbsp all-purpose flour). So, if a recipe says a 4-egg quantity, use 4 eggs, 100 g / 4 oz caster sugar (½ cup sugar) and 100 g / 4 oz plain flour (1 cup all-purpose flour). For larger mixtures (greater than 4-egg quantity), it is necessary to whisk the mixture for 10 minutes over hot water, and then up to 5 minutes off the heat to achieve the required consistency. The finished cake in each case will be about 5–6 cm / 2–2½ in deep.

For the very large cakes (25 cm / 10 in and upwards), I suggest preparing and cooking the mixture in two halves. This is practical for several reasons. First, you would need an extremely large mixing bowl to mix the quantity of eggs. Secondly, the volume is frequently reduced when large amounts are mixed. The baking time is very short if the mixture is made like a sandwich cake – only 15–20 minutes for each cake. Finally, it is more than likely that you would split a large cake and sandwich it together with some sort of filling.

Genoese sponge

This is basically a whisked sponge cake, but melted butter is added after the flour to give a more moist, richer cake, which has improved keeping qualities. To make a slightly softer sponge, some of the flour is replaced by cornflour.

Basic recipe:

3 eggs
½ cup − 1 tbsp / 75 g / 3 oz caster sugar
½ cup all-purpose / 65 g / 2½ oz plain flour
2 tbsp / 15 g / ½ oz cornflour (cornstarch)
3 tbsp / 40 g / 1½ oz butter, melted and cooled

Follow the method given for whisked sponge cake, but fold in the melted butter after the flour. Bake as for whisked sponge.

Whisked sponge mixtures chart

Egg quantity and tin size	Oven temperature	Approx. cooking time
2-egg quantity fills:		
2 × 18 cm / 7 in sandwich tins	190°C / 375°F / Gas 5	10–15 minutes
20 sponge drops or fingers	200°C / 400°F / Gas 6	7–8 minutes
15 cm / 6 in round tin	190°C / 375°F / Gas 5	25 minutes
3-egg quantity fills:		
2 × 20 cm / 8 in sandwich	190°C / 375°F / Gas 5	10–15 minutes
18 × 7 in round tin or 15 cm / 6 in square tin	190°C / 375°F / Gas 5	30–35 minutes
Swiss roll tin: 34 × 24 cm / 13½ × 9½ in	220°C / 425°F / Gas 7	7–8 minutes
900 g / 2 lb (1.7 litres / 2¾ pt) loaf tin	190°C / 375°F / Gas 5	20–25 minutes
23 cm / 9 in (1.5 litres / 2½ pt) ring tin	190°C / 375°F / Gas 5	20–25 minutes
4-egg quantity fills:		
6 × 20 cm / 8 in discs greaseproof or waxed or non-stick paper	190°C / 375°F / Gas 5	8–10 minutes
20 cm / 8 in round tin or 18 cm / 7 in square tin	190°C / 375°F / Gas 5	30–35 minutes

For larger cakes, use the following:

Tin size	Egg quantity	Oven temperature	Approx. cooking time
23 cm / 9 in round 20 cm / 8 in square	5	190°C / 375°F / Gas 5	30–35 minutes
25 cm / 10 in round 23 cm / 9 in square	2 × 3	190°C / 375°F / Gas 5	15 minutes
28 cm / 11 in round 25 cm / 10 in square	2 × 4	190°C / 375°F / Gas 5	15 minutes
30 cm / 12 in round 28 cm / 11 in square	2 × 5	190°C / 375°F / Gas 5	15 minutes

RICH FRUIT CAKE

This is suitable for Christmas or other celebration cakes, and although it may be eaten without any icing or decoration, it is usual to cover it first with a layer of almond paste, then with a royal icing or fondant icing.

Any fruit cake improves with keeping and it is best to make it at least three months before required, although it will keep for up to a year if wrapped and stored correctly.

No alcohol is added to this cake mixture before cooking, although if you have time to soak the dried fruits in a little brandy, rum or sherry before cooking, this will plump the fruit and make the cake more moist. Fruit may be soaked for up to three days. Any spirit left over when the fruit is strained should be kept and poured over the cake once it is cooked.

Spirit can be added as frequently as wished after cooking. Simply warm a little spirit in a small saucepan. Make a series of holes in the surface of the cake with a fine skewer and pour the spirit over. Leave until completely absorbed, then wrap the cake securely in greaseproof or waxed paper and/or foil. Then place in a large airtight container or polythene bag and seal. Store in a cool dry place.

Follow the chart for quantities of ingredients and tin sizes.

Method

Line the correct cake tin with a double thickness of greaseproof or waxed paper or non-stick paper.

Sift together all the dry ingredients.

Quarter or chop the glacé cherries and mix together with all the fruits.

Cream together the butter and sugar until light and fluffy.

Add the eggs, one at a time, beating well between each addition. Add the almond essence, black treacle (molasses) and grated rind of orange and lemon with the eggs. If it looks as though the mixture is 'splitting' or 'curdling', add a large spoonful of flour and beat well to give a smooth mixture once again.

Fold in the flour and then the fruit until well mixed.

Transfer the mixture to the prepared tin and level the surface, then make a slight dip in the cake so that the outer edge is slightly higher. The cake will rise more in the centre during cooking and this counteracts that rise, giving a flatter surface to the cooked cake.

For large cakes, wrap several thicknesses of brown paper or newspaper around the tin and secure with string.

Bake in a preheated oven for the suggested time, but always check the cake about 15–30 minutes before end of cooking time, depending on the size of the cake, as all ovens vary slightly. If the cake is becoming too brown on the surface, cover it with a layer of foil, or greaseproof or waxed paper.

To test if the cake is cooked, insert a skewer into the centre of the cake. The skewer will come out clean if the cake is cooked. If the mixture is still soft and uncooked in the centre it will stick to the skewer.

Allow the cake to cool in the tin. When cold, remove from the tin and peel off the lining paper.

If wished, add some spirit at this stage. Prick the surface of the cake with a skewer. Warm a few spoonfuls of brandy or other spirit and pour over the cake. Wait until completely absorbed, then wrap the cake. The spirit can be added at frequent intervals during storage.

RICH FRUIT CAKE

RICH FRUIT CAKE CHART							
Round tin	18 cm / 7 in	20 cm / 8 in	23 cm / 9 in	25 cm / 10 in	28 cm / 11 in	30 cm / 12 in	33 cm / 13 in
Square tin	15 cm / 6 in	18 cm / 7 in	20 cm / 8 in	23 cm / 9 in	25 cm / 10 in	28 cm / 11 in	30 cm / 12 in
Ingredients							
Butter	150 g / 5 oz ½ cup + 2 tbsp	200 g / 7 oz 1 cup − 2 tbsp	300 g / 10 oz 1¼ cup	350 g / 12 oz 1½ cups	450 g / 1 lb 2 cups	550 g / 1¼ lb 2½ cups	675 g / 1½ lb 3 cups
Sugar: caster or soft brown granulated or light brown	150 g / 5 oz ⅔ cup	200 g / 7 oz 1 cup	300 g / 10 oz 1½ cups	350 g / 12 oz 1⅔ cups	450 g / 1 lb 2¼ cups	550 g / 1¼ lb 3 cups	675 g / 1½ lb 3½ cups
Orange, grated rind of	½	½	1	1	1	1½	2
Lemon, grated rind of	½	½	1	1	1	1½	2
Black treacle (molasses)	½ tbsp	½ tbsp	1 tbsp	1 tbsp	1 tbsp	1½ tbsp	2 tbsp
Almond essence (almond extract)	½ tsp	½ tsp	1 tsp	1 tsp	1 tsp	1½ tsp	2 tsp
Eggs	3	4	5	6	9	12	14
Flour, plain (all-purpose)	175 g / 6 oz 1½ cups	225 g / 8 oz 2 cups	375 g / 13 oz 3¼ cups	450 g / 1 lb 4 cups	550 g / 1¼ lb 5 cups	675 g / 1½ lb 6 cups	850 g / 1 lb 14 oz 7¼ cups
Mixed spice, ground (apple pie spice)	½ tsp	¾ tsp	1 tsp	1½ tsp	2 tsp	2½ tsp	3 tsp
Cinnamon, ground	¼ tsp	½ tsp	¾ tsp	1 tsp	1¼ tsp	1½ tsp	1½ tsp
Nutmeg, ground	¼ tsp	½ tsp	¾ tsp	1 tsp	1¼ tsp	1½ tsp	1½ tsp
Salt	½ tsp	¾ tsp	1 tsp	1 tsp	1 tsp	1½ tsp	2 tsp
Currants	200 g / 7 oz 1¼ cups	300 g / 10 oz 1⅔ cups	425 g / 15 oz 2½ cups	500 g / 1 lb 2 oz 3 cups	625 g / 1 lb 6 oz 3⅔ cups	800 g / 1¾ lb 4⅔ cups	1 kg / 2¼ lb 6 cups
Sultanas (seedless white raisins)	175 g / 6 oz 1 cup	225 g / 8 oz 1⅓ cups	375 g / 13 oz 2 cups + 2 tbsp	425 g / 15 oz 2½ cups	550 g / 1¼ lb 3⅓ cups	675 g / 1½ lb 4 cups	850 g / 1 lb 14 oz 5 cups
Raisins	175 g / 6 oz 1 cup	225 g / 8 oz 1⅓ cups	375 g / 13 oz 2 cups + 2 tbsp	425 g / 15 oz 2½ cups	550 g / 1¼ lb 3⅓ cups	675 g / 1½ lb 4 cups	850 g / 1 lb 14 oz 5 cups
Glacé cherries (candied cherries)	75 g / 3 oz bare ¼ cup	100 g / 4 oz ½ cup	150 g / 5 oz ⅔ cup	175 g / 6 oz ¾ cup	225 g / 8 oz bare 1 cup	300 g / 10 oz 1¼ cups	350 g / 12 oz bare 1½ cups
Cut mixed peel	50 g / 2 oz ½ cup	60 g / 2½ oz ⅔ cup	75 g / 3 oz ¾ cup	100 g / 4 oz 1 cup	150 g / 5 oz 1¼ cups	200 g / 7 oz 1¾ cups	275 g / 9 oz generous 2 cups

Oven temperature 150°C / 300°F / Gas 2, reducing to 140°C / 275°F / Gas 1 halfway through cooking for the larger cakes (25 cm / 10 in and above).

Cooking time (hours)	2–2½	2–2½	2–2½	3–3¼	3–3½	3½–3¾	4–4¼

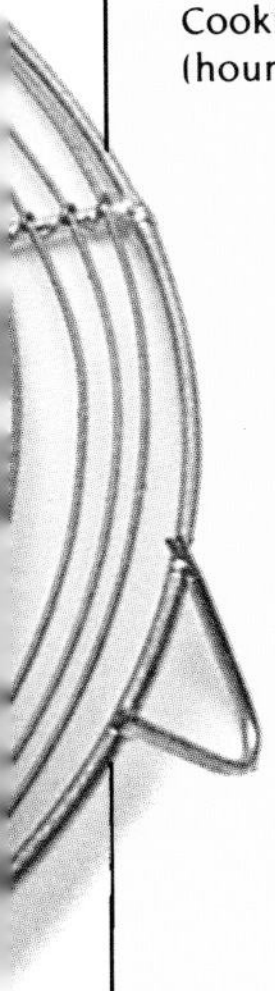

Use almonds (whole, blanched, rubbed or flaked), preferably toasted; hazelnuts (whole, blanched or chopped), preferably toasted;

shelled walnut halves; shelled pecan halves and shelled and skinned pistachios (whole or chopped).

To toast nuts, either place

on a baking sheet in an even layer and put under a medium grill, turning from time to time, until evenly browned, or place in the oven at 180°C / 350°F /

Gas 4 for about 10 minutes until evenly browned. This is also the way to loosen skins from hazelnuts. After toasting, allow the nuts to cool a little,

then place them in a paper bag and rub between the palms of your hands until the skins flake off.

To skin pistachios, almonds

and walnuts, bring to the boil in a minimum of cold water, drain immediately and drop into cold water. Drain again. With almonds, simply rub the

skins off. For pistachios and walnuts use a small sharp knife to remove the skins. Leave the nuts to dry on kitchen paper.

Coconut: is available as desiccated (shredded) or as long thread. It is useful for coating the sides of cakes. It may be toasted to a light golden colour by placing in a shallow tin and baking at 180°C / 350°F / Gas 4 for 10 minutes.

Small biscuits may be used to cover the sides of cakes or to give an extra decoration to the top of a cake, e.g. florentines, langues de chats, brandy snaps, cigarellas.

Chocolate coffee beans have a chocolate centre or a liquid coffee centre. Chocolate vermicelli is useful for coating the sides of cakes.

Crystallized rose and violet petals are commercially prepared and sold loose or in small tubs. Mimosa balls are small yellow flowers of the Mimosa bush, alsoi commercially crystallized.

Dragées are available in silver and other colours.

Small sweets or candies look particularly good on children's novelty cakes.

Icing flowers are commercially made flowers available from specialist suppliers and are sold individually.

Leaves, such as scented geranium, lemon balm and strawberry, may be used as decoration, either plain or sugared.

Chocolate decorations can be made at home (page 54), but small pieces of chocolate or chocolate sweets may be used as decoration, too.

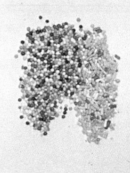

Sugar strands, hundreds and thousands, etc., are available in tubs from supermarkets.

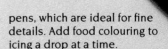

Apart from glacé cherries, angelica and ginger, there are many crystallized fruits, such as pineapple, apple, orange, fig, pear, apricot and clementine, available either in boxes or loose, from specialist confectioners.

Edible food colourings are available in liquid and paste form, as well as in felt-tipped pens, which are ideal for fine details. Add food colouring to icing a drop at a time.

Fresh fruit

The colours and textures of fruits, especially soft fruits and some of the tropical varieties, finish off a cake beautifully. Take care in preparation to make even-shaped pieces and brush with apricot or redcurrant glaze when using fruit as a complete covering to stop it drying out. Single pieces of fruit need not be glazed when used as additional decoration. Drained, canned fruit can also be used when fresh fruit is unavailable.

Cherries and redcurrants
Use on or off the stem, either plain or sugared.

Orange segments
Cut the white pith away from the orange with the peel. Use a sharp knife to remove each segment from the skin which holds the orange together. You can also make twists from orange, lime and lemon slices.

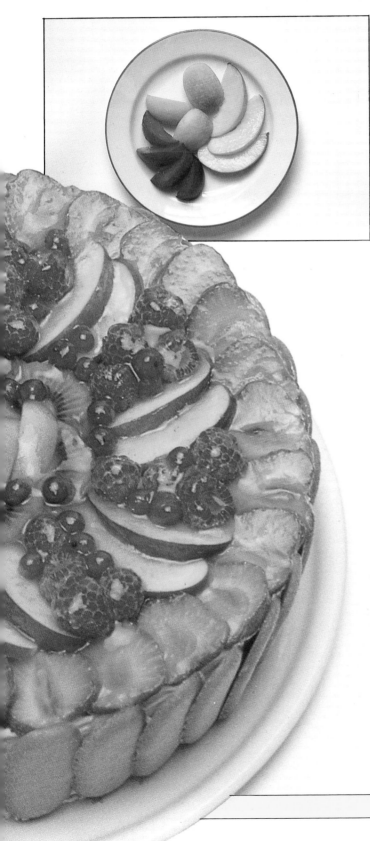

Julienne strips of orange, lemon or lime
Pare the rind from the fruit with a vegetable peeler and cut into very fine strips with a sharp knife or pair of scissors. If wished, bring to the boil in cold water, drain at once and plunge into cold water, drain again and dry on kitchen paper.

Peaches, nectarines and plums
Slice and dip in lemon juice to prevent discoloration.

Strawberries and raspberries
Use whole, hulled or unhulled, halved or sliced.
  Remember to dip sliced banana and apple in lemon juice to prevent discoloration.

Non-edible decorations

When time is limited, very pretty results can be achieved with ribbons and bought decorations. Sections of doily can be attached to the side of a cake with dabs of icing, then finished with a ribbon to give a pretty frill. Fresh or fabric flowers and leaves make an instant simple decoration.

Silver decorations. Bells, leaves, horseshoes, ribbons and keys are available from stationers and department stores for special occasion cakes. Some gilt decorations are available as well.

Green leaves and dried asparagus fern. Leaves made from fine paper and wire are available, as well as dried asparagus fern. These may be used with moulded flowers for a bouquet or spray.

Fluffy animals, such as chicks and rabbits, are available from stationers. These are particularly appropriate on Easter or novelty cakes.

Candles and holders. Available from supermarkets and stationers, these are made in an infinite variety of shapes and colours.

Sugared flowers. Whole fresh flowers look very pretty on a cake and they can be given a crystallized look by painting them with a little lightly beaten egg white and then sprinkling with caster sugar. They should be left to dry until hardened. Roses are particularly suitable, but other flowers may also be used.

Ribbons and braids useful to tie round the sides of a cake.

Paper doilies. May be cut and used to make cake frills.

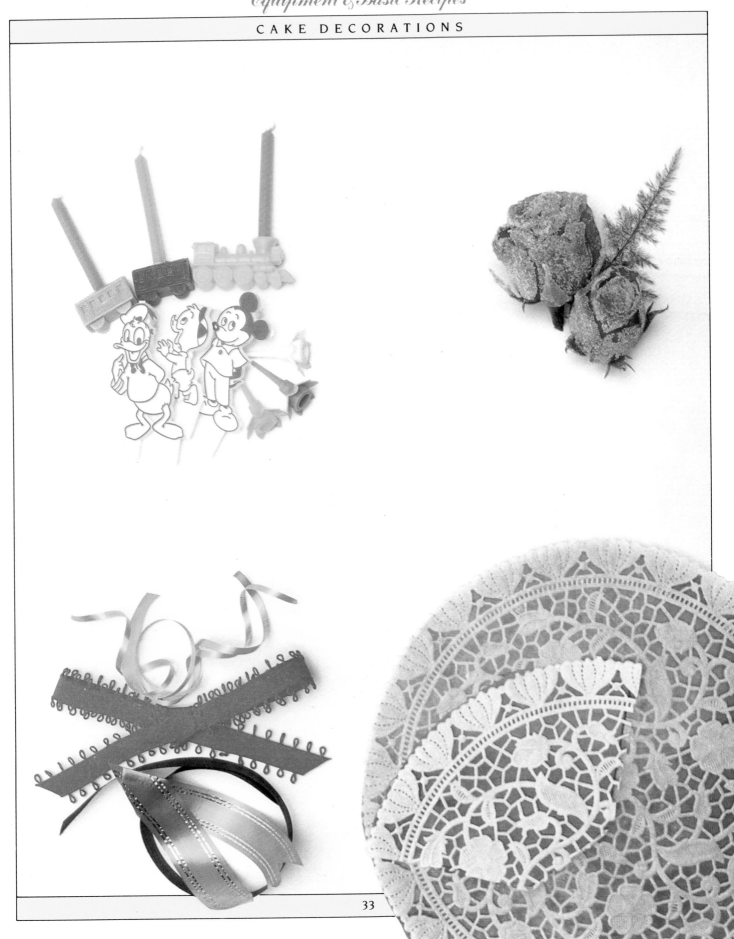

Useful basic recipes

Apricot glaze

This is frequently spread over a sponge or sandwich cake before the layer of icing is applied. The sticky glaze ensures there are no loose crumbs that could stick to the icing and spoil the finished effect. It is also used to attach decorations to a cake, such as desiccated coconut or chopped nuts, to attach almond paste to a rich fruit cake, and as a glaze for fresh fruits on a gateau.

¾ cup / 225 g / 8 oz apricot jam

2 tbsp water

squeeze of lemon juice

Place the jam, water and lemon juice in a small saucepan. Heat gently until the jam has dissolved, then boil for 1 minute. Strain and cool.

Any spare glaze can be stored in the refrigerator in a screw-top jar for several weeks. Warm the glaze gently to re-use.

Variation

REDCURRANT GLAZE. Replace the apricot jam with redcurrant jelly. Omit water. No need to strain.

Stock syrup

This is simply sugar dissolved in water, which can be flavoured with liqueur or spirit, and is used to moisten sponge layers before assembling them with fresh cream or icing. It is also used to soften fondant icing so that it can be poured over a cake. Stock syrup may be stored in the refrigerator for several weeks in a screw-top jar or other container.

½ cup / 100 g / 4 oz granulated sugar

⅔ cup / 150 ml / ¼ pt water

Place the sugar and water in a saucepan and dissolve gently. Bring to the boil and boil for 1 minute. Flavour with any liqueur or spirit to the desired strength.

Praline

A delicious mixture of whole, unblanched almonds toasted with sugar to form a caramel. The caramel is usually finely chopped or ground and may be used as a decoration, or to flavour butter creams or fresh whipped cream.

¾ cup / 100 g / 4 oz unblanched whole almonds

½ cup / 100 g / 4 oz caster sugar

Place the almonds and sugar in a saucepan over a very low heat. Stir continually until the nuts are toasted and the sugar has caramelized to a rich golden colour. Lightly butter or oil a baking sheet and pour the praline over the sheet. Leave until completely cold, then break into pieces.

Finely chop or grind the praline, or place in a thick plastic bag and pound it with a rolling pin. The praline may then be sieved if wished, but I prefer a slightly coarser texture. Store in an airtight container.

Apricot glaze

Redcurrant glaze

Caramel

Sugar syrup can be boiled until it reaches a golden caramel colour. Once this has set hard it can be broken into tiny pieces and used very effectively as a decoration. With a gas hob it is possible to put only sugar into a pan and heat it gently until caramelized. But with an electric hob, I find this more difficult, so it is better to make a strong sugar syrup first and then boil it to a caramel stage.

½ cup / 100 g / 4 oz caster or granulated sugar

3 tbsp water

Dissolve the sugar in the water in a saucepan over gentle heat. Bring to the boil and boil to a golden caramel. Pour onto a buttered or oiled baking sheet and leave until set hard. Break into tiny pieces. This does not store well, so make only sufficient for the decoration.

Caramel may also be used as a coating, rather like an icing. In this case, pour it directly onto the sponge layer and leave until starting to set. Mark out the portions of the cake with an oiled knife, otherwise the cake will be impossible to cut when the caramel is hard.

Stock syrup

Praline

Caramel

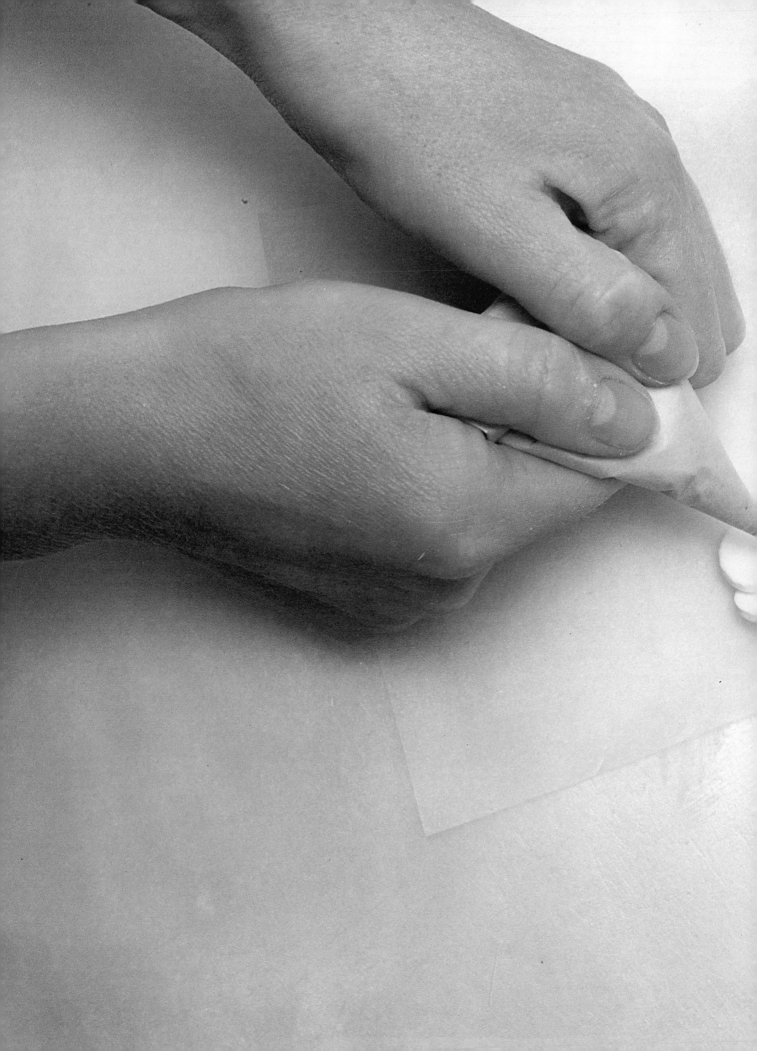

There are many different cake icings which are easy to make and require no special equipment to make them. Some are suitable for a simple sponge while others transform that simple sponge into an elaborate gâteau. The techniques of applying the icings are given under each type and full instructions are given for piping and moulding decorations. So, whether you have a sandwich cake or a rich fruit cake to decorate, there are many ideas on the following pages, ranging from the easiest to the more challenging.

Icing Recipes & Techniques

Glacé icing

This is the simplest of all icings. It can be flavoured with coffee or chocolate to give a richness and density that white icing lacks. It can also be coloured by adding a few drops of edible food colouring. When poured directly over a cake, glacé icing gives a smooth shiny coating that sets hard on the surface while remaining soft underneath. The coating may be left undecorated, or piped with designs in contrasting coloured glacé icing or butter cream.

Butter creams

These are soft, creamy icings made from butter. The simplest one is made from butter and icing sugar beaten together until light and fluffy. French butter cream (crème au beurre) is a smooth, pipeable icing made with unsalted butter. Marshmallow butter creams are particularly light and fluffy.

Butter creams are used as fillings as well as icings, and are frequently spread over the sides of a cake to hold a side decoration, such as chopped nuts, grated chocolate or desiccated coconut. They also pipe very well.

Fudge icings and frostings

These are made from a variety of ingredients, frequently incorporating egg whites, butter, sugar and cream. The similarity between these two groups is that they are mixed over direct heat or hot water, or have the basis of a hot sugar syrup. The icings are therefore very soft and can be swirled to give a decorative effect. Once cold they set firm on the surface, remaining soft underneath.

Chocolate icings

A simple icing in itself, chocolate can also be mixed in many ways to give deliciously rich icings. Melted chocolate can also be used effectively to decorate cakes.

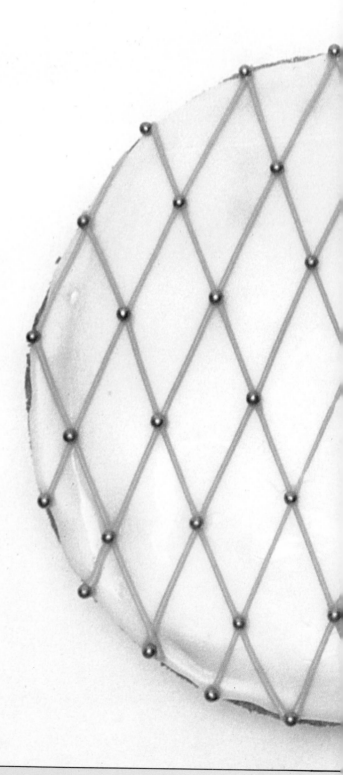

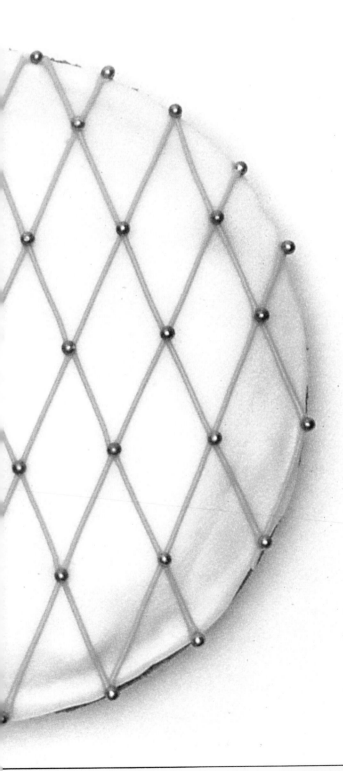

Moulding icings

Traditional fondant icing is perhaps the most difficult moulding icing to make, but it is extremely versatile. It is made from a sugar syrup that is boiled to a precise temperature (a sugar thermometer is invaluable), then cooled by working it with a palette knife until it can be kneaded by hand. The resulting icing is opaque white, which hardens as it cools, but, unlike royal icing, it remains soft to the bite. The icing can be rolled out or softened to a pouring consistency with a little extra sugar syrup and poured directly over a cake. It gives a very good finish to a cake and extra decoration can be made by piping the thickened fondant or using a firmer mixture for moulding shapes.

There is an easy fondant recipe, which requires no cooking and can be used in the same way as the traditional fondant. Commercially prepared fondant is also available from most supermarkets and cake decorating suppliers.

The other moulding icings are much simpler alternatives to traditional fondant, but they can be used in the same way.

Almond paste (marzipan)

This is a mixture of ground almonds and sugar mixed together with beaten egg. Almond essence or orange flower water may be added to heighten the flavour. It is sometimes used on its own as a cake covering and, if wished, toasted to give an attractive finish. Almond paste is particularly good for modelling shapes. It absorbs most colours well, but because it is basically yellow in colour some food colourings do not give a good final result. A whiter paste can be made by adding egg whites only to bind the mixture.

Royal icing

The traditional icing for rich fruit cakes, royal icing sets hard with a matt finish. It can be made several weeks in advance and used as required. It is made from sifted icing sugar mixed with egg whites; lemon juice is added to ensure a good white colour and glycerine gives a softer texture. It can be peaked to give a quick decorative effect, but it is usually used as a smooth flat surface on which to pipe elaborate designs in a slightly firmer royal icing.

Apart from icings, there are many simple yet highly effective ways of decorating a cake, using whipped cream, meringue or dredged icing sugar.

Decorating with fresh cream

Fresh cream makes a very good filling and 'icing' for a whisked sponge cake, transforming it into something quite special.

Double cream (USA: whipping cream or heavy cream) is the best cream to use as it whips well and holds its shape when piped. Whipping cream has a lower fat content and is less firm than double cream. It can be used for spreading, but is not as good for piping. There are commercial cream substitutes in powder form, which pipe very well when reconstituted with milk.

Both cream and cream substitutes are piped through a large star nozzle rather than the smaller icing nozzles.

Whipped cream may be used as the finished covering of a cake. For the sides it can be smoothed or serrated using an icing comb, or used as a base for another covering, such as chopped nuts or langues de chats biscuits. The addition of fresh fruit on the top of the cake adds colour and texture. The fruit can be arranged on the surface and glazed with apricot or redcurrant glaze (page 34), then piped with whirls of whipped cream, or the cream can be the main decoration with a little fruit for added colour.

To whip fresh cream

Place the cream in a bowl and, using a hand-held electric mixer or a balloon whisk, whisk the cream until it forms soft peaks. Be careful not to overwhip the cream as it will become very thick and granules will appear. This texture cannot be remedied.

Decorating with meringue

Meringue mixture pipes very well and effectively, and can be used in a similar way to fresh cream as a decoration. It should be browned very quickly for 2–3 minutes in a preheated oven set at the hottest setting. Any other decoration, such as whipped cream or fresh fruit, should be added afterwards.

Basic recipe
2 egg whites
pinch salt
½ cup / 100 g / 4 oz caster sugar

Whisk the egg whites with the salt until stiff. Add the sugar a spoonful at a time, whisking thoroughly between each addition until a thick white meringue mixture is formed. Use at once.

TO USE. Spread the sides of the cake with a thin layer of meringue. A thicker layer can be used as insulation for an ice-cream filling.

Spread the top of the cake with an even layer. Place the remaining mixture in a nylon piping bag fitted with a large star nozzle and pipe a decorative pattern.

Place the cake in a preheated oven for 2–3 minutes until golden. Add any further decorations.

A meringue-covered cake is best eaten straightaway, but if it has an ice-cream filling, it can be kept in the freezer for an hour or two until ready to serve.

Decorating with icing sugar

Dredged icing sugar is the easiest decorative topping. Spoon a little icing sugar into a sieve and sprinkle it over the surface of the cake. Use a palette knife to lightly score the surface with diagonal lines to create a simple pattern.

More elaborate results can be achieved by sprinkling the icing sugar over a doily, then carefully removing it.

Cocoa powder or drinking chocolate powder can be used as a second sprinkling to give a more intricate design.

GLACE ICING

This very simple icing is used to decorate sandwich or sponge cakes, but it is also useful when decorating pastries and biscuits or cookies. It may be coloured with edible food colourings and flavoured in many ways. If adding a liquid flavouring, such as a liqueur, omit an equivalent amount of the water. The quantity given in the basic recipe will cover the top and sides of a 20 cm / 8 in cake; use half the quantity for the top only.

Basic recipe

2 cups / 225 g / 8 oz icing sugar, sifted
2 tbsp warm water

Sift the sugar into a bowl and add the warm water. Beat well until smooth and thick enough to coat the back of a wooden spoon. Add a little extra liquid if necessary. If you add too much liquid, simply sift in more sugar to achieve the required consistency. Use at once.

Variations

Liquid flavourings must be used in place of water and *not* in addition.

VANILLA. Use 1 tsp vanilla essence in place of the same amount of water.

ORANGE, LEMON, LIME, GRAPEFRUIT OR OTHER FRUIT JUICE. Substitute strained fruit juice for the measured amount of water.

COFFEE. Dissolve 1 tbsp instant coffee powder in the measured water.

CHOCOLATE. Substitute 2 tbsp sifted cocoa powder for an equal quantity of icing sugar.

LIQUEUR. Substitute liqueur for an equal amount of water. Use at least 1 tbsp liqueur, but increase this if wished.

COLOURED. Add a few drops of the appropriate edible food colouring.

Using glacé icing

Apart from its use as a coating, glacé icing may be piped, using a plain or writing nozzle (no. 2 or no. 3). However, it is not firm enough to make rosettes and whirls. Piped rosettes or swirls of butter cream may be added to an iced cake for further decoration.

To coat the top of a cake

Place the cake on a plate or board. If desired, brush the top with a thin layer of apricot glaze (page 34).

Pour or spoon the icing on to the centre of the cake. Using a palette knife, spread the icing carefully to the edges. Dip the clean palette knife in hot water and smooth the icing.

Tap the plate gently on the work surface to release any air bubbles and give a smooth finish. Any small air bubbles may be burst with a pin. Leave to set for at least 1 hour.

An alternative method of coating the top of a cake is to make a greaseproof or waxed paper collar about 1 cm / ½ in deeper than the cake. Wrap the collar tightly round the cake and secure with a paper clip. Pour the icing on to the cake and spread to the edges. Leave icing to set before carefully removing the collar.

If decorations are to be added, press these into the icing before it sets completely. If further piped icing is desired, pipe this when the base coat is completely set.

To coat the top and sides of a cake

Follow the basic rules for coating the top, but allow the icing to flow down the sides and carefully smooth it with a wetted palette knife. Once the icing is set the excess may be scraped from the plate or board. An alternative method is to place the cake on a wire rack over a plate or piece of greaseproof or waxed paper, and allow the excess icing to drip through. Once the icing is set, the cake can be carefully removed from the rack.

Quilted icing

Use a no. 2 or no. 3 plain or writing nozzle and pipe parallel lines 1–2 cm / ½–¾ in apart over the set base coat. Always start with a central line and pipe either side of it. Turn the cake and pipe another series of parallel lines at an angle to the first, thus producing a diamond pattern.

Press a small flower or dragée on to the icing at each intersection. Leave to set. Contrasting coloured icings should be used to give a bold effect.

Feather icing

Make the glacé icing and reserve about 2 tbsp. Colour this a contrasting colour or, if liked, colour each tablespoon of icing a different colour.

Make one or two small greaseproof paper piping bags (page 18) and insert a no. 2 or no. 3 plain or writing nozzle. Fill with the reserved icing.

Coat the top of the cake with remaining icing. While still wet, pipe parallel lines in coloured icing, about 2.5 cm / 1 in apart, across the cake. Using a skewer or wooden cocktail stick, *quickly* draw it across the cake at right angles to the piped lines. Turn the cake and draw the skewer in the opposite direction between the first series of markings. Leave to set.

Cobweb icing

Follow the directions for feather icing above, but instead of parallel lines, pipe circles of icing about 2.5 cm / 1 in apart. Draw the skewer across the piped lines at regular intervals, starting at the outside edge and working towards the centre. If desired, draw the skewer in the opposite direction between the first series of markings. Leave to set.

These are perhaps the most versatile icings for sponge and sandwich cakes as they can be used for filling and topping a cake, as well as covering the sides as a base for decoration. They pipe well and are easily flavoured and coloured. Butter gives a better flavour, but margarine may be used if wished. The basic recipe will fill and cover the top of a 20 cm / 8 in sandwich cake, or cover top and sides.

Basic butter cream

½ cup / 100 g / 4 oz butter, at room temperature
2 cups confectioners' / 225 g / 8 oz icing sugar, sifted
1–2 tbsp milk or 1 large egg yolk (optional)

Beat the butter until light and fluffy, then beat in the icing sugar a little at a time until well mixed. If wished, beat in the milk or egg yolk to give a richer icing.

If not required immediately, store in an airtight container in the refrigerator. Leave in a warm place to soften slightly before use.

Creme au beurre

A deliciously rich, smooth butter cream. Always use unsalted butter as salted butter gives too strong a flavour. This quantity will fill and top a 20 cm / 8 in sandwich cake plus extra for piped decorations.

½ cup – 1 tbsp / 75 g / 3 oz granulated sugar
4 tbsp water
2 egg yolks
¾ cup / 175 g / 6 oz unsalted butter

Place the sugar in a saucepan with the water and heat gently until dissolved. Bring to the boil and boil until the temperature reaches 108°C / 226°F on a sugar thermometer.

Beat the egg yolks in a bowl until pale. Pour the syrup in a thin stream on to the egg yolks, whisking all the time. Continue to whisk until the mixture is thick and cold.

Beat the butter until light and fluffy. Gradually beat the egg mixture into the butter until evenly blended.

Use at once to fill and decorate.

Variations for butter cream and crème au beurre

VANILLA. Add 1–2 tsp vanilla essence to taste.

PEPPERMINT. Add 1–2 tsp peppermint essence to taste and colour with green edible food colouring.

LEMON, ORANGE, LIME OR GRAPEFRUIT. Add 1–2 tbsp strained fruit juice, and grated rind if wished. Colouring may also be added.

CHOCOLATE. Add up to 4 squares / 100 g / 4 oz / melted and cooled chocolate, or 4 tbsp sifted cocoa powder.

COFFEE. Add 1–2 tbsp instant coffee powder dissolved in 1–2 tbsp hot water, or use coffee essence.

FRUIT PURÉE. Add up to generous ½ cup / 100 ml / 4 fl oz very thick fruit purée, such as strawberry, raspberry, apricot or blackcurrant.

LIQUEUR. Add up to 2 tbsp of the chosen liqueur.

Marshmallow butter cream

A light and fluffy icing made by beating softened butter into a meringue mixture. The meringue may be made either by whisking egg whites and icing sugar over simmering water until stiff, or by boiling a sugar syrup to the hard ball stage and adding that to stiffly whisked egg whites. Both versions can be flavoured in the same way as butter cream and crème au beurre.

Recipe 1: sufficient to fill and top a 20 cm / 8 in sandwich cake

2 egg whites
1 cup confectioners' / 125 g / 4 oz icing sugar, sifted
½ cup + 2 tbsp / 150 g / 5 oz butter, softened

Place the egg whites and sugar in a bowl over a pan of simmering water. Whisk for 5–7 minutes until the mixture is thick and white. Remove from the heat and continue whisking until cool.
    Beat the butter until fluffy, then fold in the meringue mixture.
    Flavour as desired and use at once.

Recipe 2: sufficient to fill and cover a 20–23 cm / 8–9 in cake

1 cup / 225 g / 8 oz granulated sugar
½ cup / 100 ml / 4 fl oz water
4 egg whites
1 cup / 225 g / 8 oz butter, softened

Place the sugar and water in a saucepan and heat gently until dissolved. Bring to the boil, and boil until the syrup reaches the hard ball stage on a sugar thermometer: 121°C / 250°F.
    Meanwhile, whisk the egg whites until stiff. As soon as the syrup is ready, pour it in a thin stream on to the egg whites, whisking all the time. Continue to whisk until the mixture stands in stiff peaks. Leave to cool.
    Beat the butter until fluffy, then fold in the meringue mixture.
    Flavour as desired and use at once.

Variations
Recipe 1
LEMON AND ORANGE. Add grated rind ½ lemon or orange and 1 tbsp juice.
CHOCOLATE. Add 2 squares / 50 g / 2 oz melted chocolate, cooled.
COFFEE. Add 2–3 tsp coffee essence or instant coffee powder dissolved in a little hot water.
PRALINE. Add 3–4 tbsp praline (page 35).
Recipe 2
Use up to double the amount of the above flavourings.

Fondant Butter Cream

This is a good way of using up leftover fondant icing. It has a creamy texture similar to crème au beurre. The quantity given is sufficient to fill and cover a 20 cm / 8 in cake.

¾ cup / 175 g / 6 oz fondant (page 58)
1–2 tbsp stock syrup (page 34)
¾ cup / 175 g / 6 oz butter, softened

Warm the fondant with the syrup, in a bowl over hot water, until it is soft enough to beat.
    Beat the butter until fluffy, then beat in the cooled fondant.
    Flavour as desired (see above) and use at once.

To decorate the sides of a cake

The sides of a cake may be spread with a butter cream, then left smooth, swirled with a knife or combed with an icing comb. If, however, a further coating, such as chopped nuts, is required the cake may first be spread with either apricot glaze or butter cream. For gâteaux, crème au beurre or fresh cream is usually used.

Spread the sides of the cake with a thin layer of butter cream or brush with apricot glaze.

Spread the chosen coating on a sheet of greaseproof or waxed paper and, holding the cake between the palms of your hands, gently roll it over the coating until evenly covered.

Sometimes a cake may be too delicate for this, in which case, the coating ingredient must be pressed against the sides of the cake using a palette knife.

Suitable coatings include: chopped nuts; toasted coconut; chocolate vermicelli; grated or chopped chocolate.

BUTTER CREAMS

Butter cream is a smooth spreadable icing, which can be easily made into an effective pattern.

Spread an even layer over the cake then:

1. Use a fork to make a circular design on a round cake, or straight or wavy lines on a square cake. If wished, mark the cake into sections with a knife.
2. Using a palette knife, work the icing from side to side, slightly overlapping the lines made by the knife each time.
3. Using a palette knife, start from the centre of the cake and make swirls to the edge, each time overlapping the previous swirl.
4. Use a palette knife to make a general swirling pattern.

Butter cream also pipes very well and can be used in many ways to give a decorative effect. For more information on piping techniques, see page 84.

Using a star nozzle, pipe one of the following designs:
1. Straight parallel lines in one or more contrasting colours.
2. Rosettes in lines or circles, in one or more contrasting colours.
3. Large shells or rosettes around the edge of the cake.
4. A lattice effect over the surface of the cake.
5. Scrolls on each marked portion of the cake.
6. Pipe elongated loops from the centre to the outside edge of the cake and fill each loop with jam.

1

2

3

4

1

2

3

4

5

6

FUDGE ICINGS

These icings are very soft and can be swirled easily to give a decorative effect. Once cold, they set firm on the surface, yet remain soft underneath.

The basic recipe is a smooth fudge icing that turns golden during cooking, so don't worry and think you've spoiled it! It is sufficient to cover an 18–20 cm / 7–8 in ring cake or a 20 cm / 8 in sandwich cake.

generous ½ cup / 150 ml / ¼ pt single (half-and-half) or soured cream
1 cup + 2 tbsp / 225 g / 8 oz caster sugar
½ cup / 100 g / 4 oz unsalted butter

Place the cream and sugar in a saucepan and heat very gently until dissolved.

Increase the heat and boil the mixture for about 15 minutes, until it reaches the soft ball stage on a sugar thermometer: 116°C / 240°F. Stir frequently to prevent the mixture sticking to the pan. If you don't have a sugar thermometer, a small spoonful of the mixture should form a soft ball when dropped into cold water.

Leave to cool for about 2 minutes, then beat in the butter, a little at a time. If the icing starts to look oily, add an ice cube and beat vigorously until it has melted; this will return the icing to a good consistency.

Coat the cake immediately, allowing the icing to run down the sides and using a palette knife as little as possible, or allow to thicken and spread over the cake.

Variations
CHOCOLATE. Beat in 2 squares / 50 g / 2 oz plain chocolate, broken in pieces, with the butter.
NUT. Beat in ¼–½ cup / 25–50 g / 1–2 oz finely chopped toasted nuts.
COFFEE. Beat in 1 tbsp instant coffee powder dissolved in 1 tsp hot water.

Lemon fudge icing

Sufficient to cover an 18 cm / 7 in cake

3 tbsp / 40 g / 1½ oz butter

2 tbsp lemon juice

1⅔ cup confectioners' / 225 g / 8 oz icing sugar, sifted

grated rind ½ lemon

Melt the butter and the lemon juice in a saucepan over a gentle heat. Bring to the boil. Remove from the heat, add the sugar and lemon rind and beat well. Allow to cool slightly, then use at once.

Variations

CARAMEL. Substitute milk and brown sugar for the lemon juice and icing sugar. Omit lemon rind.

COFFEE. Substitute milk for the lemon juice; add 1 tbsp instant coffee powder. Omit lemon rind.

CHOCOLATE. Substitute milk for the lemon juice; add 1–2 tbsp cocoa powder. Omit lemon rind.

ORANGE OR LIME. Substitute orange or lime juice and rind for the lemon juice and rind.

These have the texture of marshmallow and they spread and swirl easily. They set quickly so have your utensils and cake decorations ready before you start.

American frosting

This frosting is easily flavoured and coloured. In order to make it successfully, however, it is best to use a sugar thermometer. The quantity given is sufficient to cover the top and sides of a 23 cm / 9 in sandwich cake. Half quantity is sufficient to cover a 23 cm / 9 in ring cake.

1½ cups / 350 g / 12 oz granulated sugar
⅔ cup / 150 ml / ¼ pt water
2 egg whites
pinch salt or cream of tartar

Place the sugar and water in a saucepan and heat gently until dissolved.

Bring to the boil and boil steadily, without stirring, for about 10–15 minutes until a sugar thermometer registers the soft ball stage: 116°C / 240°F. Remove the sugar syrup from the heat.

Whisk the egg whites with the salt until stiff. Slowly pour the sugar syrup on to the egg whites, whisking all the time until cool and thick. As this takes 5–10 minutes, it is best to use a hand-held electric mixer.

Add any chosen flavourings and colourings, and use at once.

Variations

LEMON OR OTHER CITRUS FRUITS. Beat in grated rind of a medium lemon with 1 tbsp juice. Add a few drops of edible food colouring if desired.

COFFEE. Whisk in 2 tbsp instant coffee powder dissolved in 2 tsp hot water.

CHOCOLATE. Whisk in 4 tbsp cocoa powder dissolved in 2 tbsp hot water.

VANILLA, PEPPERMINT OR ALMOND. Whisk in 2–3 tsp of the appropriate essence. Add a few drops of green food colouring with the peppermint essence, if wished.

CARAMEL. Substitute soft brown sugar for the granulated sugar.

Seven-minute frosting

This gets its name from the fact that it takes seven minutes to make! It is similar in texture to American frosting, but can be made without a sugar thermometer. Sufficient to cover an 18–20 cm / 7–8 in cake.

1 egg white
¾ cup / 175 g / 6 oz caster sugar or soft brown sugar
2 tbsp hot water
pinch salt or cream of tartar

Put all the ingredients in a bowl over a saucepan of hot water.

Whisk until the mixture thickens sufficiently to stand in soft peaks; this should take about 7 minutes using a hand-held electric mixer. Use at once.

Variations

Any flavourings should be added at the beginning with all the other ingredients. Follow the flavours for American frosting, but use only *half* the amount.

Jam frosting

This is a very much reduced sugar icing for those who are more calorie conscious! Do not make this too far in advance of using and eating, as it is not as stable as those frostings with a lot of added sugar. Sufficient to cover a 20 cm / 8 in cake.

3 egg whites
pinch salt
4 tbsp jam, warmed and sieved

Whisk the egg whites and salt until stiff enough to stand in peaks. Whisk in the jam and continue to whisk for a further minute.

CHOCOLATE ICINGS

There are many different chocolate icings to make, but the easiest one is simply melted chocolate, though this does set hard and is rather difficult to cut unless you use a hot knife.

Very simple, but still very rich icings can be made by just adding a little butter or fresh cream to melted chocolate. This softens the chocolate, making it more manageable and sometimes suitable for piping. Spirit, particularly rum, is often added.

Butter cream and crème au beurre may be flavoured with melted chocolate (page 43), and glacé icing can be made with some sifted cocoa powder in addition to the icing sugar (page 40).

What kind of chocolate to use

There are many types of chocolate available and it may be confusing when it comes to deciding which one you should use for what purpose. Basically, chocolate can be divided into three categories.

1. CHOCOLATE CAKE COVERING. This is usually found in the baking section of the supermarket. It is not a true chocolate bar, but melts and spreads easily and is perfectly acceptable for everyday and children's cakes. It is also slightly softer in texture than a true chocolate bar and is, therefore, easier to grate or to make into chocolate curls.

2. COOKING CHOCOLATE. This is available in bars and as drops. It is very good for all icings and chocolate cookery.

3. SUPERIOR DESSERT CHOCOLATE. An expensive choice, which should be used only for very special icings.

Ganache

This is one of the richest chocolate icings imaginable! It is made from chocolate and double cream, which are melted together, then mixed to a dark, smooth icing. It can be spread as it is, or whipped to lighten it and increase the volume. Liqueur or spirit may be added as desired. Once whipped, ganache pipes extremely well. The quantity given is sufficient to fill and cover a 20 cm / 8 in cake.

I cup whipping / 250 ml / 8 fl oz double cream
8 squares semisweet / 225 g / 8 oz plain chocolate

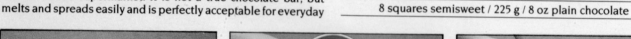

Chocolate frosting

Heat the cream to just below boiling. Remove from the heat.

Break the chocolate into small pieces and add to the cream. Leave for several minutes until the chocolate has melted. Beat well, then leave to cool.

If wished, whip the cooled chocolate icing until pale and doubled in bulk. Add spirit as desired. Use at once.

Mocha icing

This is a very dark chocolate icing, flavoured with coffee. Pour over a cake and allow it to flow down the sides. Use a palette knife as little as possible to spread it and it will set to a glorious shine. The quantity given is sufficient to cover a 20–23 cm / 8–9 in cake.

½ cup / 100 g / 4 oz caster sugar
3 tbsp cocoa powder
2 tbsp water
1 tsp instant coffee powder
6 tbsp / 75 g / 3 oz butter

Heat the sugar, cocoa, water and coffee in a saucepan over a gentle heat, stirring all the time with a wooden spoon, until the sugar has dissolved. Bring to the boil and simmer for 1 minute, Remove from the heat.

Beat in the butter and allow to cool sufficiently to coat the back of a wooden spoon. Use at once.

Chocolate frosting

This is a spreadable icing that can be swirled to give a decorative, yet quick finish to a cake. The quantity given is sufficient to cover a 20 cm / 8 in cake.

4 squares semisweet / 100 g / 4 oz plain or milk chocolate
2 tbsp / 25 g / 1 oz butter
5 tbsp milk
2–2¼ cups confectioners' / 300 g / 10 oz icing sugar

Melt the chocolate and butter in the milk in a saucepan over a gentle heat. Add the icing sugar and beat well. Allow to cool.

Mocha icing

DECORATING WITH CHOCOLATE

Melted chocolate can be used very effectively to decorate a cake and several ideas are shown here. No doubt you will think of many others as you experiment.

Chocolate decorations can give a really professional finish to any cake. Small decorations can be piped on to non-stick paper, left to set, then carefully peeled off and transferred to the cake. Run-outs can be made in a similar way to that described for royal icing (page 90).

Many of these decorations can also be piped freehand on to a cake. Practise first on a plate – the chocolate can be collected up and remelted. Do remember to let the chocolate cool as much as possible before piping it.

Most chocolate decorations can be made in advance and kept for several weeks in a rigid airtight container, between sheets of greaseproof or waxed, or non-stick paper. Store in a cool place or the refrigerator.

To melt chocolate

Place some broken pieces of chocolate in a small bowl over a saucepan of simmering water until melted. Do not use more heat than is necessary and stir as little as possible.

To pipe melted chocolate

Make a small paper piping bag (page 18) and pour the chocolate directly into it. Fold in the sides and fold over the top to seal it. Snip off a tiny piece at the tip and pipe directly on to the iced cake, or pipe shapes and designs on to non-stick paper.

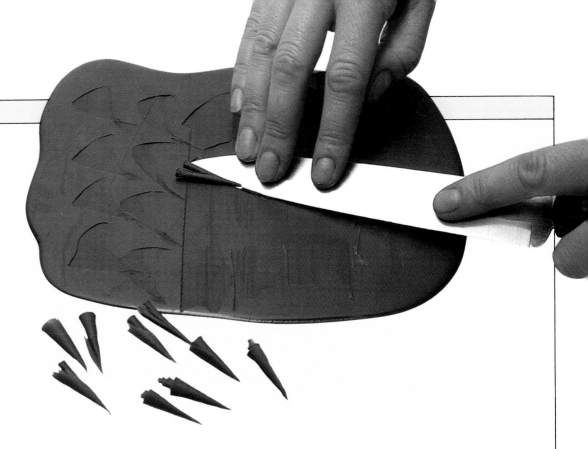

COMBED CHOCOLATE. This is done directly on to the cake. Spread the surface of the cake with melted chocolate and when beginning to firm, use an icing comb or fork to produce a pattern. Draw the comb across the chocolate in straight or wavy lines.

EASY CHOCOLATE CURLS. Use a vegetable peeler to scrape curls from a chocolate bar.

CHOCOLATE CARAQUE. Melt some chocolate and spread evenly on a piece of marble or plastic laminate. Leave to set. Using a sharp knife, held at a 45° angle to the chocolate, scrape the knife away from you across the surface of the chocolate to make long chocolate curls. This takes some practice, but produces superior curls. Ragged-edged petals can be made by using a small sharp knife and rotating it over the surface of the chocolate.

DECORATING WITH CHOCOLATE

CHOPPED OR GRATED CHOCOLATE. Finely chop or grate the chocolate on a coarse grater.

CHOCOLATE SHAPES. These are made from melted chocolate that has been spread thinly and left to harden.

Melt the chocolate. Secure a piece of non-stick paper to a baking sheet with a dab of chocolate, then spread the chocolate evenly. Tap the tray to level the surface of the chocolate, then leave in a cool place (not the refrigerator) to set.

When just set, stamp out shapes using warmed cutters, or cut squares, triangles and other shapes freehand with a warm sharp knife. Leave until completely firm. Gently ease off the paper with a palette knife, then store until required.

Contrasting chocolate may be piped on these shapes to give a more decorative finish.

PIPED CHOCOLATE DECORATIONS. Fill a small piping bag with chocolate and pipe lacy shapes on non-stick. Leave to set, then peel off the paper and store until required. Many decorations can be piped directly onto the cake. However, they need to be piped on paper if you want them to stand up, or to arrange them in rosettes of cream or butter cream icing.

CHOCOLATE CONES. Make tiny non-stick paper cones, from 10 cm / 4 in squares, in the same way as you would make a piping bag.

Using an artist's paintbrush, brush the inside of each cone with chocolate. Leave to set. Paint a second coat of chocolate for added strength. Leave to set, then carefully peel away the paper. If you wish to level the top edge of the cone, very carefully press it on to a just warm cake tin or baking sheet. The cones may be filled with fresh cream or butter cream.

CHOCOLATE LEAVES. Wash and dry rose leaves or fresh bay leaves. Paint the undersurface of each leaf with melted chocolate and leave to set, chocolate side up. Carefully peel away the leaf and you will be left with a chocolate replica.

CHOCOLATE RUN-OUTS. Draw a template of the required shape and place it under a square of non-stick paper so that the outline shows through. Pipe the outline in chocolate and allow it to set. Carefully fill the centre of the outline with melted chocolate, easing it into the corners with a skewer or cocktail stick. Tap the tray gently on the work surface to remove any ridges from the chocolate. Leave to set completely, then carefully remove from the paper and store.

For butterflies 'in flight', fold the non-stick paper along the 'body line'. After piping, leave to set, supported at a 90° angle, in a small square container.

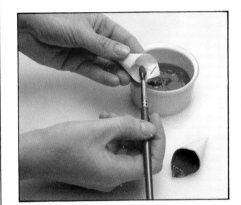

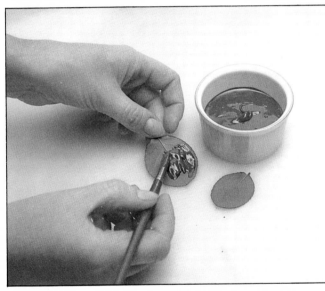

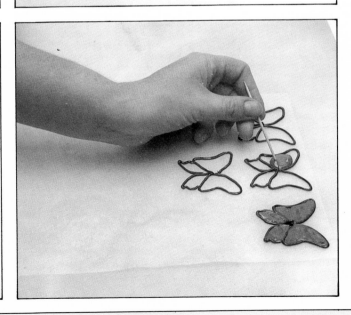

These icings are extremely versatile as they can be used for covering a cake and for moulding or modelling handmade decorations.

Boiled fondant icing

Known as the traditional fondant icing, this is basically a sugar syrup to which liquid glucose is added – this stops large sugar crystals forming as the syrup goes cold. A sugar thermometer is necessary to make this icing correctly. It may be poured in its thickened liquid state over a cake and left to set. It can also be kneaded to a malleable stage, then rolled out and used to cover a cake or moulded into flowers and other decorative shapes.

The finished fondant may be stored in an airtight container in the refrigerator for several weeks. To use it, simply warm a little stock syrup (page 34) with the fondant to achieve the correct consistency. This is best done in a bowl over a saucepan of simmering water. Colourings should be added at this stage.

The quantity given is sufficient to cover a 20 cm / 8 in cake.

2 cups / 450 g / 1 lb granulated sugar
⅔ cup / 150 ml / ¼ pt water
1 tbsp liquid glucose
flavouring and colouring as desired

Place the sugar and water in a saucepan and dissolve over a gentle heat. Keep a small bowl of cold water and a pastry brush to hand, and from time to time brush around the inside of the pan just above the level of the syrup to prevent any sugar crystallization.

Add the liquid glucose. Bring the syrup to the boil and boil, without stirring, until it reaches the soft ball stage on a sugar thermometer: 116°C / 240°F. Immediately remove from the heat. To ensure the syrup does not get any hotter, place the saucepan in a shallow bowl of iced water.

For a *pouring consistency*, beat the syrup with a wooden spoon until it becomes opaque and thick enough to coat the back of a wooden spoon. Add any colourings or flavourings at this stage.

Pour immediately over a cake that has been brushed with apricot glaze (page 34). If the cake is placed on a wire rack over a plate or baking sheet, any spare icing (free of crumbs) can be collected and rewarmed for further use.

For a *kneading consistency*, it is best to have a wetted marble slab. Pour the cooled syrup on to the slab, a little at a time, and work it continually with a large palette knife in a 'paddling' movement, until it is opaque and cool enough to handle. Knead the fondant well, then store in an airtight container until required. Colourings can be kneaded in before use, but flavourings should be added while the syrup is still liquid.

Variations

COFFEE. Add 1 tbsp coffee essence or 1 tbsp instant coffee powder dissolved in 1 tsp hot water.
CHOCOLATE. Add 2 squares / 50 g / 2 oz melted chocolate, cooled.
COLOURED. Add several drops of edible food colouring and stir in at the syrup stage or knead into the finished icing.

Easy fondant icing

This fondant requires no cooking and can be used in the same way as kneaded boiled fondant icing. The quantity given will cover a 20 cm / 8 in cake.

4 cups confectioners' / 500 g / 1 lb 2 oz icing sugar, sifted
1 egg white
2 tbsp liquid glucose, warmed
edible food colouring (optional)

Place most of the sugar in a bowl. Make a well in the centre and add the egg white and glucose.

Beat the mixture with a wooden spoon, or work it with your hands to make a firm paste, adding extra sugar as required.

Place fondant on a work surface lightly sprinkled with icing sugar and knead in a few drops of edible food colouring. Store as for boiled fondant icing.

Satin icing

This is very similar to easy fondant icing, but the fat content gives it a particularly smooth finish, hence its name. The quantity given is sufficient to cover a 23 cm / 9 in cake.

4 tbsp / 50 g / 2 oz butter, margarine or white fat (shortening)
2 tbsp lemon juice
2 tbsp water
about 4½–5 cups confectioners' / about 675 g / 1½ lb icing sugar, sifted
few drops edible food colouring (optional)

Put the fat and liquids in a saucepan and heat gently until the fat has melted. Add about one-third of the sugar and stir over a low heat until dissolved. Increase the heat slightly and cook until the mixture just begins to boil. Remove from the heat.

Stir in another one-third of the sugar and beat well until evenly mixed. Turn the mixture into a mixing bowl.

Add sufficient of the remaining sugar to mix to a firm paste. Dust the work surface with icing sugar and knead the icing until smooth.

Add a few drops of food colouring, if wished, and knead well until evenly coloured. Wrap in a polythene bag or cling film, and place in an airtight plastic container. The icing will keep for several weeks in the refrigerator. To use, allow to soften at room temperature and knead until smooth.

Mallow paste

This icing sets firm and is particularly good for modelling or moulding flowers. The quantity given is sufficient to cover an 18 cm / 7 in cake.

| 2 tsp gelatine (gelatin) |
| 2 tsp white fat (shortening) |
| 3 tbsp water |
| About 3½ cups confectioners' / 500 g / 1 lb 2 oz icing sugar, sifted |
| edible food colouring (optional) |

Place the gelatine, fat and water in a bowl over a saucepan of simmering water and heat gently until dissolved. Pour mixture over three-quarters of the sugar in a bowl and work together with fingertips until a smooth paste is formed, adding as much of the remaining sugar as necessary.

Colour as wished and store as for satin icing.

To cover a cake with moulding icing

Apart from coating a cake with boiled fondant icing in its liquid state, moulding icings may be rolled out and placed straight on to a cake that has been glazed with apricot glaze or covered with a base layer of almond paste.

To use, dust the work surface lightly with icing sugar. Roll out the icing to a round or rectangle about 5 cm / 2 in larger all round than the top of the cake.

Dust your hands with icing sugar or cornflour, then carefully lift the icing on to the cake with the aid of a rolling pin. Starting from the centre of the cake, smooth the icing over the top and sides. Trim off excess icing and leave to dry out for 3–4 hours.

For a rectangular cake, it is easier to cut away a triangle of icing at each corner so that the icing will lie flat.

Trimmings may be reserved for decoration. Wrap them in polythene or cling film to prevent them drying out. Small balls of icing may be rolled and arranged around the base of the cake to neaten the edge.

Handmade decorations in moulding icings

Moulding icings are soft, pliable icings that can be easily shaped. Their great advantage over almond paste is that they are white and therefore very useful in their basic state. They can, however, be coloured with edible food colours as wished. To colour the icings, simply knead a little chosen colouring into the icing until completely blended and even in colour. To prevent the icings drying out before use, wrap in polythene and keep in an airtight container.

When moulding and rolling out, it's a good idea to dust fingers with a light sprinkling of cornflour. Also, dip cutters in cornflour before stamping out shapes.

Once made, decorations should be laid on non-stick paper on a baking sheet and left to dry, uncovered, in a warm place for 1–2 days.

CHRISTMAS ROSES. Roll out white icing on a surface lightly sprinkled with icing sugar or cornflour. Stamp out five plain rounds with a small cutter or the end of a plain nozzle. Pinch each round together at one side to form the petals. Arrange the petals against the sides of a plate or patty tin so that they dry in a curved position. When completely dry, attach the petals to one another with a little royal icing. Leave to dry, on non-stick paper, then pipe little dots of yellow royal icing around the centre for stamens.

PANSIES. Use purple or yellow icing. For each flower roll out four and stamp out small circles and one larger one. Pinch each circle at one side and leave to dry. When firm stick the four smaller petals together in pairs, overlapping each other slightly. Attach the larger petal at the bottom. Leave to dry, then paint fine streaks of edible food colouring in a contrasting colour.

MICHAELMAS DAISIES. Use purple icing. Roll out and stamp out a small fluted round, then, using a cocktail stick, press all round the edge to give a petal effect. Pipe dots of yellow royal icing in the centre. For buds, fold the round into an attractive shape.

DAFFODILS. Use yellow or orange icing. To make a trumpet, cut a small rectangle of icing. Press a cocktail stick along one long edge to flute it. Roll it into a cylinder, then squeeze one end together.

Cut out six petals for each flower. Carefully attach these round the base of each trumpet with a little unbeaten egg white. Shape the petals for a more realistic effect. If wished, paint the top of each trumpet with a little orange food colouring.

ROSES. Use any suitable colour. Mould a small piece of icing into a cone shape. Press or stamp out small circles for the petals. Wrap each petal round the cone and secure with a little egg white. Curve or roll the tops of the petals outwards. For small roses, four or five petals will be sufficient; buds need only two or three petals tightly wrapped round the cone.

Many other decorations, such as animals and figures, may be made using moulding icings. See pages 68–75 for more ideas.

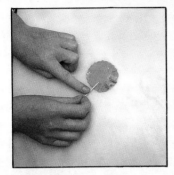

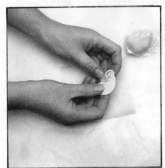

Sparkling sugar bells make a very attractive decoration on casually iced cakes, covered with frosting or peaked royal icing. They can be made well in advance and stored for several months very successfully.

Sugared or crystallized flowers also make a very pretty decoration on all kinds of cakes. Choose strong-coloured flowers with a distinctive shape, such as violets, roses and primroses, as the sugar tends to soften the outline. Make sure the flowers are fresh and free from damage or brown marks.

Sugar bells
Makes about 20 small bells
¼ cup / 50 g / 2 oz granulated sugar
a little royal icing (page 78)
silver dragées

Mix the sugar with a few drops of water, making sure that the sugar is only *just* moistened. Pack the sugar in clean metal bell decorations and level the ends with the back of a knife. Tap out on to a piece of non-stick paper on a baking sheet. Repeat until the sugar is used up.

Leave until the sugar on the outside of the bells is hardened and you can pick them up without breaking them. Carefully scrape out the soft centres with a skewer to leave a bell-shaped shell. Leave overnight until completely dried out.

Pipe a line of icing from the centre of the inside of each bell to the edge and stick a silver dragée at the end for a clapper. Leave until set.

The sugar bells may be stored in an airtight container between layers of tissue paper until required.

Crystallized flowers

1 tbsp / 15 g /% ½ oz gum arabic
2 tbsp rose water
caster sugar
fresh flowers

Mix together the gum arabic and rose water and leave for about 2 hours or until the gum arabic has dissolved. Stir occasionally.

Using a fine artist's paintbrush carefully paint the petals of the flower on both sides. Leave for 15–20 minutes to allow the solution to be absorbed. Sprinkle with caster sugar until evenly coated and shake off any excess. Place on a sheet of non-stick paper on a baking sheet and leave to dry in a warm place for 1–2 days. Remove carefully and store in an airtight tin, between layers of tissue paper.

Almond paste (marzipan) is most often used as the 'undercoat' icing for a rich fruit cake. it can, however, be used on its own as an icing for fruit cakes or plain cakes, or as an 'undercoat' icing on sponge cakes which are to be covered in fondant or other moulding icings.

It is made from ground almonds, sugar and egg. The egg may be whole, beaten egg, or egg yolks or egg whites. It is perhaps more usual to use egg yolks only as the whites can then be kept to make other icings. Using egg whites does give a paler colour, which is more useful if colourings are to be added for decorating purposes.

Commercially made marzipan is available in blocks. Knead this well, adding a little egg, if necessary, to soften it to a suitable consistency. Use as a convenient alternative to homemade.

Almond paste contains a lot of oil and it must be allowed to dry completely before a white icing is used as a covering. Allow about one week before applying royal icing. The quantity given in the basic recipe makes about 900 g / 2 lb almond paste.

Basic recipe

2⅔ cups / 450 g / 1 lb ground almonds
2 cups/ 450 g / 1 lb caster sugar (or use half caster and half icing sugar /half granulated and half confectioners' sugar
about 2 eggs, beaten, or 4 egg yolks or whites
2 tsp lemon juice
1 tsp almond essence

Mix the ground almonds and sugar in a large bowl. If using icing sugar, sift it first to remove any lumps.

Add three-quarters of the egg with the lemon juice and almond essence, and work to a smooth paste, adding more egg as required.

Turn out on to a work surface sprinkled with a little icing sugar and knead until smooth. Wrap in cling film or polythene and store in the refrigerator until required.

To cover a cake with almond paste

Almond paste is usually applied to the top and sides of a cake. If the top is not level, trim it and, if wished, turn it upside down. If the cake sides are too well cooked, trim to level them.

Measure the circumference and depth of the cake to be covered. The easiest way to do this is to cut a piece of string for each of these measurements.

Take a generous half of the almond paste and on a surface lightly sprinkled with icing sugar, roll out a strip of almond paste the depth and circumference of the cake, using the two pieces of string as a guide. If the cake is very large, cut two strips. Trim to the exact measurements.

Roll out the remaining almond paste to a circle or square the exact size of the top of the cake. Trim to size.

Brush the almond paste pieces or the cake sides with apricot glaze (page 34). Hold the cake between the palms of your hands and press it firmly on to the almond paste. Continue rolling or turning the cake until the almond paste is attached. Press gently all round and neaten the join.

Brush the top of the cake with apricot glaze and either place the cut shape of almond paste on top of the cake and press gently, or invert the cake on to the paste and press gently on the base to ensure the paste is attached. Using a palette knife, smooth the join all round the cake to neaten.

Carefully place the cake, right side up, on a board and leave to dry for at least a week before coating with royal or fondant icing. This is very important because the oil in the paste will seep through the icing and cause brown staining if it is not properly dried, and this cannot be rectified.

Quantities of almond paste required to cover top and sides of round and square cakes
These quantities allow a generous layer of almond paste; obviously less may be used.

Size of cake	Quantity of almond paste
15 cm / 6 in square 18 cm / 7 in round	450 g / 1 lb
18 cm / 7 in square 20 cm / 8 in round	675 g / 1½ lb
20 cm / 8 in square 23 cm / 9 in round	900 g / 2 lb
23 cm / 9 in square 25 cm / 10 in round	1.2 kg / 2½ lb
25 cm / 10 in square 28 cm / 11 in round	1.4 kg / 3 lb
28 cm / 11 in square 30 cm / 12 in round	1.6 kg / 3½ lb
30 cm / 12 in square	1.8 kg / 4 lb

Icing Recipes & Techniques

ALMOND PASTE DECORATIONS

Almond paste (marzipan) is a very easy mixture to work with and can be modelled into shapes, such as fruit, or rolled out and stamped with shaped cutters. It absorbs edible food colouring very well, although its basic yellow colour (more pronounced in commercially produced pastes) may distort some colours. For example, purple colouring can result in a greyish finish. However, there are now many makes of superior colourings, mainly in paste form, which give very good results.

It is important to make any decorations to a sensible scale for the cake on which they are to be used. Figures and animals will generally require between 25 g / I oz and 75 g / 3 oz of paste. The Father Christmas and the choir boy shown on page 00 take about 25 g / I oz and the larger animals, such as the elephant, use about 75 g / 3 oz.

Always leave the decorations to dry on non-stick paper for a few days to prevent any oil and colouring seeping through on to white icing. Attach the decorations to the cake with a dab of icing.

Fruit and vegetables

Use real fruit and vegetables as a guide to making the moulded versions, particularly if you want to try modelling some of the more exotic varieties.

CARROTS. Shape small orange cones and paint streaks of brown with edible food colouring or make horizontal markings with a knife. Use a little green paste for the top or a small piece of pistachio nut or angelica.

CAULIFLOWER. Roll a small ball of natural paste over a coarse grater to give a rough effect. Press out or stamp out green leaves and wrap around the 'flower'.

AUBERGINE. Roll! purple paste into a pear shape, then add a small green stem.

BUNCH OF GRAPES. Roll out tiny green or purple balls and attach to a triangle of pale green paste to make the bunch. Use a clove stem to make the stalk.

APPLES. Roll out green or red balls and use some edible red or green food colouring to paint appropriate markings. Use a whole clove for the stalk.

ORANGE. Roll an orange ball over a coarse grater to give the appropriate effect. Press a whole clove into the centre.

STRAWBERRY. Make the correct shape in red paste and press on a fine grater. Use a little green paste to make the hull.

PLUM. Use purple paste and shape into an oval, mark a line with the point of a knife all round to give an indentation. Use a whole clove for the stalk.

BANANA. Roll a small piece of yellow almond paste into a banana shape and using a little edible brown colouring, paint markings.

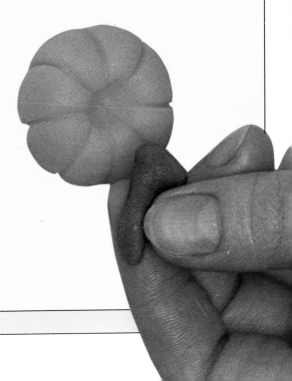

ALMOND PASTE DECORATIONS

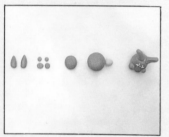  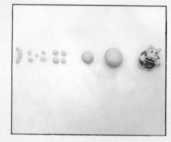 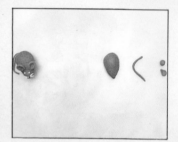

Animals

RABBIT. Follow guidelines for kangaroo, but make pointed ears and a bob tail. Pipe eyes, nose and whiskers with icing.

CAT. Reserve a small piece for the tail and roll to a suitable length, divide the remaining paste into two-thirds and one-third. Make an arch as for body of elephant and roll the smaller amount into a ball; make a cut half way through the ball to shape the ears. Attach the pieces together with a little unbeaten egg white and pipe nose, eyes and whiskers with royal icing.

TIGER. Use the kangaroo as a guide, but reserve a little paste to make a roll for the tail and make two more small balls which are flattened and marked with a skewer for the tiger's face. The body and head should be oval. Pipe all over the body and tail with stripes of chocolate as well as piping the eyes.

MOUSE. Reserve two tiny circles for the ears and pinch together at one end to make a point. Roll a long, thin length of paste for a tail. Roll the remaining paste into a pear shape with a pointed end. Attach the pieces together with a little unbeaten egg white. Leave to dry, then pipe eyes, nose and whiskers with royal icing.

ELEPHANT. Use about two-thirds of the paste for the body. Roll into a thick cylinder and arch it so that it will stand up. Cut a small indentation at the front and back of the arch to make the legs. Press out two small circles for the ears and a tiny piece for the tail; shape the remaining paste into the head and trunk. Press lines into the trunk with a sharp knife and two holes in the end of the trunk for the nostrils. Attach the pieces together with a little unbeaten egg white and leave to dry. Pipe eyes with chocolate.

KANGAROO. Make three tiny balls: two for ears and one for nose. Make two medium-sized balls for the paws and two slightly larger balls for the feet and one for a tiny pouch. Divide the remaining paste into three-quarters and one-quarter. Roll each into an oval shape for the body and head. Flatten the two feet slightly and mark indentations in each, then attach to the body with a little unbeaten egg white. Mark two horizontal lines on the head; press two small balls to shape the ears and attach to the head. Press the nose into place. Attach the head. Mark indentations on the paws and attach in place. Attach the pouch. Leave to dry, then pipe the eyes with royal icing or chocolate.

CHICKEN – Make two small wings, then divide remaining paste into two-thirds and one-third. Shape each one into an egg shape with a pointed end. Cut a small horizontal line in the point of the smaller ball for the beak. Attach the two pieces with a little unbeaten egg white and paint the inside of the beak orange. Pipe eyes with edible food colouring, royal icing or chocolate. Attach wings.

PIG. Roll three-quarters of the paste into a ball. Make two tiny circles for the ears and bring them together at one end to form a point; roll another tiny piece into a curly tail. Use the remaining paste for the snout; shape into a ball, then completely flatten one side. Make two large holes for the nostrils and cut a horizontal line for the mouth. Attach the pieces together with a little unbeaten egg white and leave to dry. Pipe eyes with a little royal icing or chocolate.

Assorted shapes

As well as being moulded into shapes, almond paste can also be stamped out with metal cutters or cut out from a template or freehand. Leaves, candles, stars and many other shapes may be made like this. Decorate with piped royal icing to give more definition to the outline.

Full instructions for making
the shapes shown here are
given overleaf.

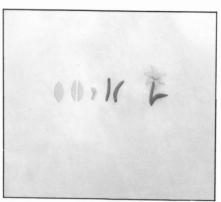
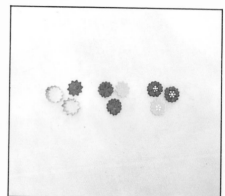

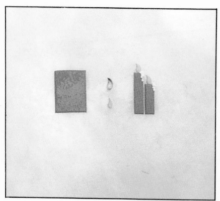
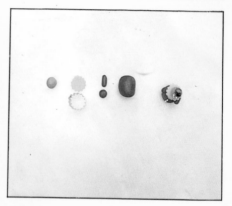

ROSE. Use any suitable colour and green for the leaves. Make a small cone as the centre of each rose, then press out or stamp out small circles of paste as the petals. Using a little unbeaten egg white press each petal on to the cone centre, shaping it around the cone. Continue attaching petals, curving them slightly to give a realistic effect. Roses can be made in graduating sizes, depending on their use.

DAFFODIL. Use yellow or orange paste. To make the 'trumpet' cut a small rectangle of paste and roll it, squeezing one end together. Cut out six petals for each flower and carefully attach these to each 'trumpet', shaping them a little to give a realistic look. If wished, paint a little orange colour on the top of each trumpet.

PRIMROSE. Stamp out small fluted circles from yellow, pink, purple or red paste. With a small knife cut indentations in 5 places evenly around each circle to make the petals. Paint orange dots in the centre with edible food colouring or pipe royal icing dots.

VIOLET. Press out or stamp out 5 purple circles for petals. Press the sides of one petal together, then attach the remaining petals, curving them slightly to make the flower shape. Use a small piece of yellow paste for the centre.

MUSHROOMS AND TOADSTOOLS. Shape a stalk from a small cylinder of paste and make the cap from a small ball of paste. Flatten one side of the cap and attach to the stalk. When dry pipe dots on the top of the cap with royal icing or chocolate.

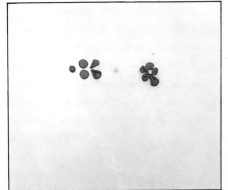  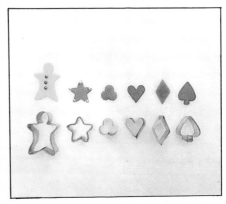

LEAVES. Roll out green paste and stamp out or cut out required shape of leaf. Use a small, sharp knife to mark veins.

CUT OUT SHAPES. Many other shapes can be stamped out in almond paste. Use a cutter or work freehand.

CHRISTMAS TREES. Make a green conical shape and use scissors to snip at frequent intervals for 'branches'. If wished, use a little brown or red paste for the tunk or holder.

CHOIR BOY. Stamp out the frill with a small fluted cutter. Make a small pink ball for the head, then use red for the body and arms. Attach pieces together with a little royal icing. Pipe dots for face and buttons. Mark hair with an icing pen.

FATHER CHRISTMAS. Make body, arms and hat in red paste and use a small pink ball for face. Pipe beard, buttons and top of hat with royal icing. Mark face with an icing pen. Follow picture for sack and toys, if wished.

CANDLES. Cut out freehand candles and flames (or use a cutter). Pipe royal icing for the 'melted wax'.

LADYBIRD. Make a red oval shape and flatten the base. Make markings with a small sharp knife and pipe eyes and dots with chocolate or royal icing.

ALMOND PASTE MARQUETRY

This is a very effective way to decorate a cake and though it looks very elaborate, it is quite simple to produce. It is based on the ideas of marquetry and mosaics used in furniture and tile design.

Small pieces of different coloured almond paste are arranged in an interlocking pattern to cover the top of a cake. Any design you like can be used and it is a good idea to draw it first. Cut a piece of paper the exact size of the top of the cake, then draw the design on it, deciding how many colours you are going to use and marking the shapes with the appropriate colour. Make a copy of the finished design on greaseproof or waxed paper and cut it into the individual pieces. Arrange these on the original pattern until you are ready to cut out the pieces.

Colour the almond paste by simply kneading a little edible food colouring into each piece. Have some apricot glaze ready to attach the pieces to the cake.

The sides of the cake should be decorated first; this can be done with one continuous strip of almond paste, or two half strips. Follow the method for covering a cake with almond paste on page 66, or cover with butter cream and a coating such as praline.

Roll out one piece of coloured almond paste on a surface lightly dusted with icing sugar or cornflour and cut out all the pieces in that colour. Repeat with the other colours, then build up the pattern on the cake, attaching each piece with a little apricot glaze and ensuring that all the pieces interlock neatly.

Royal icing

Royal icing is a hard-setting icing that is used to cover special occasion cakes. It dries quite quickly and should be kept in a bowl covered with a damp cloth when in use, and kept in an airtight polythene container in the refrigerator when stored. It is best to make it at least one day before required. This allows time for it to 'rest' and any air bubbles may be beaten out with a wooden spoon.

The consistency of royal icing varies a little with its use. For covering a cake it should be fairly firm, and just stand in peaks if pulled up with a spoon or knife. It may need thickening slightly with a little extra icing sugar for piping, and thinning with a little unbeaten egg white if used to 'flood' piped designs (see run-outs, page 90). The quantity given in the basic recipe makes about 900 g / 2 lb of icing, which is enough to cover a 20 cm / 8 in round cake. Follow the chart on page 80 for other cake sizes.

Basic recipe

4 egg whites

6½ cups confectioners' / 900 g / 2 lb icing sugar, sifted

1 tbsp lemon juice

2 tsp glycerine

Lightly whisk the egg whites in a bowl until just frothy.

Add the icing sugar, a spoonful at a time, beating well between each addition. Use either a wooden spoon or a hand-held electric mixer.

When half the icing sugar has been added, beat in the lemon juice. Beat in the remaining icing sugar until a firm texture is reached. The icing should peak if pulled up with a spoon.

Beat in the glycerine, then transfer to an airtight polythene container. Royal icing will keep for several weeks, stored in a cool place or the refrigerator. Before using, beat well and check the consistency.

If colouring icing, it is better to colour it all in one go as it may be difficult to match up the colour later. Simply add the required edible food colouring and beat well until evenly mixed.

Quantities of royal icing required to give two coats to top and sides of a fruit cake
The g / lb quantity refers to the weight of icing sugar required.

Size of cake	Quantity of royal icing
15 cm / 6 in square 18 cm / 7 in round	550 g / 1 ¼ lb
18 cm / 7 in square 20 cm / 8 in round	675 g / 1 ½ lb
20 cm / 8 in square 23 cm / 9 in round	900 g / 2 lb
23 cm / 9 in square 25 cm / 10 in round	1 kg / 2 ¼ lb
25 cm / 10 in square 28 cm / 11 in round	1.2 kg / 2 ½ lb
28 cm / 11 in square 30 cm / 12 in round	1.4 kg / 3 lb
30 cm / 12 in square	1.6 kg / 3 ½ lb

Using royal icing

Rough or peaked icing
This gives a quick finish to cakes where time is short. It is generally used on Christmas cakes to give an 'icicle effect' to the sides of the cake, or a general 'snow covering'. The same principle may be followed using frostings. Add sufficient icing sugar so that the icing will stand in stiff peaks if pulled up with the back of a wooden spoon.

Spread icing evenly over the top and sides of the cake (already covered with almond paste). Using the tip of a round-ended knife, or a palette knife, pull up the icing at regular intervals to form peaks. Leave to set for about 8 hours.

Extra decorations, such as almond paste shapes or bought decorations should be placed in position before the icing dries.

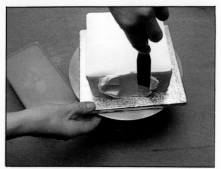

Flat icing

An even flat surface is essential on a cake that is to be piped and decorated. It is a fairly lengthy process and requires much patience and perseverance! Cakes should have a minimum of two coats of icing, but three coats give a really professional finish. The top and sides of the cake have to be iced on separate days, so that one surface is not spoiled while neatening the other. One day between each coat of icing is sufficient, so allow at least 4 days for flat icing, and this should be started about 10–14 days before the cake is required.

To flat ice the top of a cake

Place the cake (already covered with almond paste) on a board and secure with a generous dab of icing. Place the board on a non-slip work surface.

Spoon some icing on the top of the cake. Spread the icing over the top of the cake with a palette knife using a 'paddling' movement. This works out any air bubbles.

Using an icing ruler held at an angle of about 45°, draw the edge towards you over the surface of the icing in one smooth, continuous movement, taking care to press evenly but not too heavily. If the resulting surface is not sufficiently smooth, spoon a little more icing on to the cake and repeat the complete process (using a clean ruler).

Smooth off the edges of the icing by running a palette knife or plain-edged icing ruler round the top of the cake. Leave to dry.

To flat ice the sides of a cake

It is preferable to place the cake on a turntable at this stage, but if you haven't got one it is possible to improvise with a large plate over an upturned mixing bowl.

FOR A ROUND CAKE. Spread an even layer of icing all over the sides of the cake using the same paddling movement as mentioned above.

Holding a plain-edged icing comb in one hand at an angle of about 45° to the surface of the cake, and using the other hand to move the turntable slowly and evenly, start at the back of the cake and draw the comb around the icing to give a smooth finish. In effect, the icing comb is held in the same position while the free hand rotates the turntable through a full circle.

Scrape off any excess icing from the top edge and the board with a palette knife or icing comb. Leave to dry. Once dry, clean the board with a damp cloth.

FOR A SQUARE CAKE. The same basic principles apply, but there are four corners to consider, which must be kept as neat and even as possible. Beginners may find it easier to do a square cake in two stages, icing opposite sides on one day, then icing the remaining two opposite sides on the next day. If so, do allow plenty of time for this.

Spread the icing over two sides of the cake, then draw the icing comb over the surface to give a neat finish.

Using a palette knife, cut off the icing at both corners to give a neat straight edge. Trim off any excess icing and leave to dry.

Repeat the same process with the remaining two sides.

When the icing is dry, check to see how even it is. If necessary, use a clean piece of fine sandpaper to rub off any small bumps and level the surface. Remove the icing dust with a clean pastry brush.

For the second and third coats of icing, repeat the icing process once or twice more as wished, but ensure that each coat is dry before starting on the next. Leave to dry for at least 24 hours before adding any piped or moulded decorations.

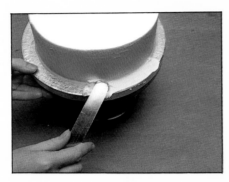 

Icing the cake board
Although the cake board is often used as it is, it may be iced as well. To do this allow the iced cake to dry completely on the board, then spread a thin layer of icing over the board, smoothing it with a palette knife. Using the same technique of rotating the turntable with one hand and holding the icing comb or palette knife in the other, smooth the icing by holding the icing comb at an angle to the board and just touching it. Neaten the edges and leave to dry.

Decorating with a serrated icing comb
A quick and attractive finish can be made using an icing comb with a serrated edge.

Flat ice the sides of the cake and leave to dry.

For the second coat use a contrasting colour of icing, if wished. Coat the sides of the cake with the icing, then, instead of smoothing the surface, draw a serrated icing comb over the sides, either in a straight or curved movement. The final effect is that of contrasting stripes. Leave to dry.

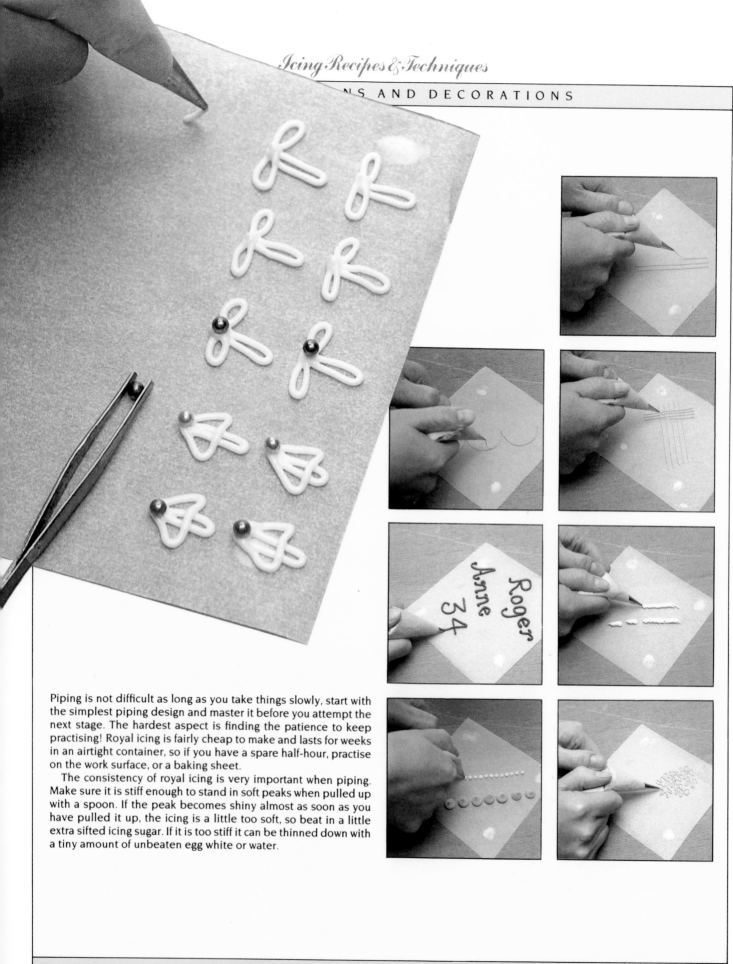

Piping is not difficult as long as you take things slowly, start with the simplest piping design and master it before you attempt the next stage. The hardest aspect is finding the patience to keep practising! Royal icing is fairly cheap to make and lasts for weeks in an airtight container, so if you have a spare half-hour, practise on the work surface, or a baking sheet.

The consistency of royal icing is very important when piping. Make sure it is stiff enough to stand in soft peaks when pulled up with a spoon. If the peak becomes shiny almost as soon as you have pulled it up, the icing is a little too soft, so beat in a little extra sifted icing sugar. If it is too stiff it can be thinned down with a tiny amount of unbeaten egg white or water.

Piping designs

Most designs are made with a plain (writing) nozzle or a star nozzle. However, there are several nozzles that make specific designs, for example, shell, basket and petal.

Make sure the nozzle tip is clean and free from icing for a neat piped line.

Using a plain nozzle (nos. 1, 2 or 3)

STRAIGHT LINES. Squeeze out the icing until it just touches the cake. Squeeze gently allowing a slightly sagging line of icing to appear from the nozzle just above the surface of the cake, at the same time pulling the piping bag towards you. Stop squeezing the icing just before the end of the line and touch the surface of the cake to finish the line and break the icing neatly.

LOOPS OR SCALLOPS. As for straight lines but following the line of a scallop (curved) design.

TRELLIS. This is a series of straight parallel lines crossed at right angles by another series of parallel lines. Always start in the centre and pipe lines to either side of this original line.

WRITING. This may be done freehand but do practise first. Icing can easily be scraped off the iced surface if an error is made. It is perhaps a good idea to make a template of the words to be written and to prick them on to the surface of the cake with a pin.

NUMBERING. This can be done in the same way as writing. Stencils will give a more professional finish, but perhaps the most bold effect can be achieved with run-outs (page 90).

ROPE. This is achieved by piping in a circular movement in a clockwise direction, piping each loop overlapping the last. The loops may be even or decreasing towards the end of the movement; this makes a leaf design.

DOTS. Simply squeeze out the icing to the required size of dot and pull the icing bag away. The points may be pressed down to give a rounded effect, or a silver ball may be pressed into each. Smaller dots of a different colour may be piped on top of the original dot.

LACE EFFECT. Hold the nozzle close to the surface of the cake and pipe a continuous wiggly line.

LACE EDGING. Pipe freehand decorative patterns. If wished they can be left to dry, then attached to the cake, overhanging the edge.

Using a star nozzle

Star nozzles come in many different sizes with a range of points. The most useful size is a no. 8, eight-pointed star.

STAR. Hold the piping bag in an upright position and with the nozzle almost on the surface of the cake, squeeze out sufficient icing to make the required size star. Pull the nozzle away quickly.

ROSETTE. This is similar to a star, but the movement is a circular one finishing in the centre of the rosette; pull away quickly.

SHELL (this can also be piped with a shell nozzle). Hold the piping bag at an angle of about 60° to the surface and squeeze out the icing to form the main shell, at the same time releasing the pressure and pulling away to form the tail.

SCROLL. This is basically a shell but the start of the scroll is made in a circular movement. Scrolls may be piped in the same direction or alternating.

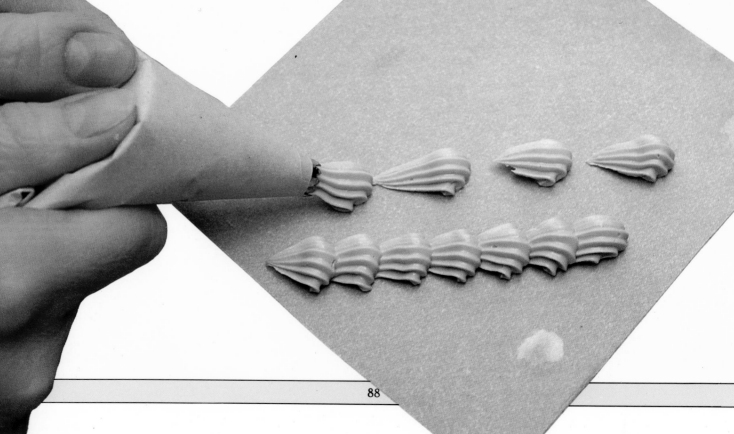

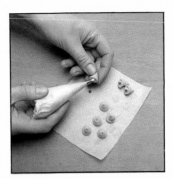

Piping decorations

BELLS. Use a no. 4 plain (writing) nozzle. Bells can be made by building up a series of dots of decreasing sizes. Pipe a large dot on a piece of waxed paper, pipe a smaller dot on top and an even smaller one on top of that one. Leave to dry until hard on the outside but soft at the base. Scoop out a little of the inside to make the bell and pipe a dot of icing inside. Press a silver dragée on to the icing.

BIRDS. Use a no. 4 plain (writing) nozzle. Pipe a large dot for the body, release the pressure, then pipe a smaller dot for the head pulling the icing away to give a point for the beak. Leave for 24 hours to dry. Pipe the wings freehand on to waxed paper using a no. I or no. 2 nozzle, and leave to dry. Attach the wings with a little icing and paint or draw eyes with edible food colouring.

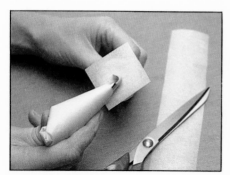
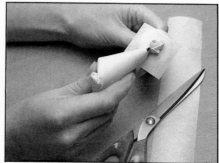
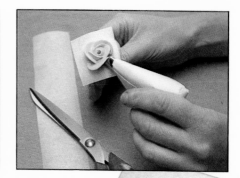

Flowers and leaves

SIMPLE FLOWERS AND FERNS. Use a no. 2 or no. 3 plain nozzle. Pipe lines for stems and pipe dots on either side of the stems for simple ferns; a ring of dots with a small dot in the centre makes a simple flower.

FLOWERS. Use a petal nozzle. There are several specific flowers which may be piped, as well as non-specific shapes. It is necessary to have an icing nail when piping these. Attach a square of non-stick paper to the icing nail with a dab of icing.

ROSE. Hold the icing nail in one hand and the piping bag with the thin part of the nozzle uppermost, in the other hand. With the nozzle in the centre of the piece of paper squeeze out a cone of icing. This will come automatically as the icing nail is slowly revolved in the thumb and forefinger. Twist the nozzle downwards to finish off the cone. To form the petals, hold the nozzle horizontally with the thin part away from you and twist the nozzle through 180°, squeezing out a little icing as you do so. Continue piping 3–5 petals in the same way always starting each one a little way back from the finish of the previous petal. Carefully lift the flaver off the icing nail and leave to dry for 24 hours, then peel off the paper and store in an airtight container until required.

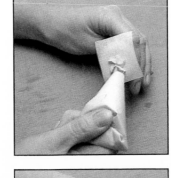
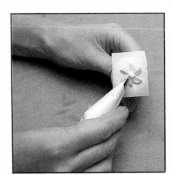

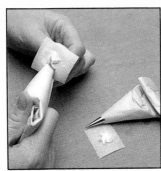
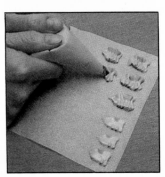

NARCISSUS OR DAFFODILS. Hold the nozzle with the thick end to the centre of the icing nail and flat to the nail. Squeeze out a little icing in the shape of a petal, repeat five more times to make the basic shape. Leave to dry. Using a small petal nozzle pipe a cone as for start of rose to make the 'trumpet'. Leave to dry. Many other blossoms and flowers may be made by piping a series of petals. They may be painted at the edge or in the centre to give a more decorative and realistic effect.

DAISY. Hold the petal nozzle with the thick part to the centre and in an upright position, and squeeze out a petal. Continue at even intervals piping a series of petals. Either pipe a dot or several dots in another colour or use a silver dragée to make the centre.

LEAVES. These may be piped with a leaf nozzle or for smaller leaves make a greaseproof paper bag and press it flat; cut a small arrow shape at the end. This will give a similar effect. Pipe out a small amount of icing, pulling away quickly as you release the pressure to give a point. A forward and backward movement will give a curly edged leaf.

Run-outs are shaped pieces of royal icing. The outline of a shape, such as a flower or bird, is first piped and left to dry. Then the shape is filled or 'flooded' with a slightly thinner icing and left for 2–3 days until completely dry.

Almost any shape can be made into a run-out, though the most usual ones are flowers, initials, numbers, bells and leaves. More elaborate run-outs can be made by tracing motifs from Christmas cards or other pictures. You can also use the trace-off templates shown at the end of the book.

To make a run-out

Trace the outline of the shape you wish to pipe on to paper. Then draw or trace that outline on to a piece of white card. Place this under a piece of non-stick paper and secure with a dab of icing.

Using a plain nozzle (no. 1 or no. 2) and the appropriate coloured icing, pipe a continuous line following the outline of the shape. Repeat this as many times as required, but always make a few extra just in case of mishap! Allow outline to dry.

Thin down some royal icing with a little lightly beaten egg white (not frothy) or water to a flowing consistency. Very carefully spoon a little icing into the centre of the outline and push it to the edges with a cocktail stick or skewer. Prick any air bubbles that appear and leave to dry for 2–3 days.

Carefully remove the shape from the paper and place in position on the cake. Secure with a little icing. Run-outs will keep for several months stored in an airtight container.

If using more than one colour in a run-out, always allow one section to dry completely before starting on the next to prevent the colours from running into each other.

Once dry, run-outs can be outlined again or extra piping can be used to improve the definition of the shape. Fine details can be painted on with liquid food colouring, or pastes thinned with a little water, or drawn with coloured icing pens.

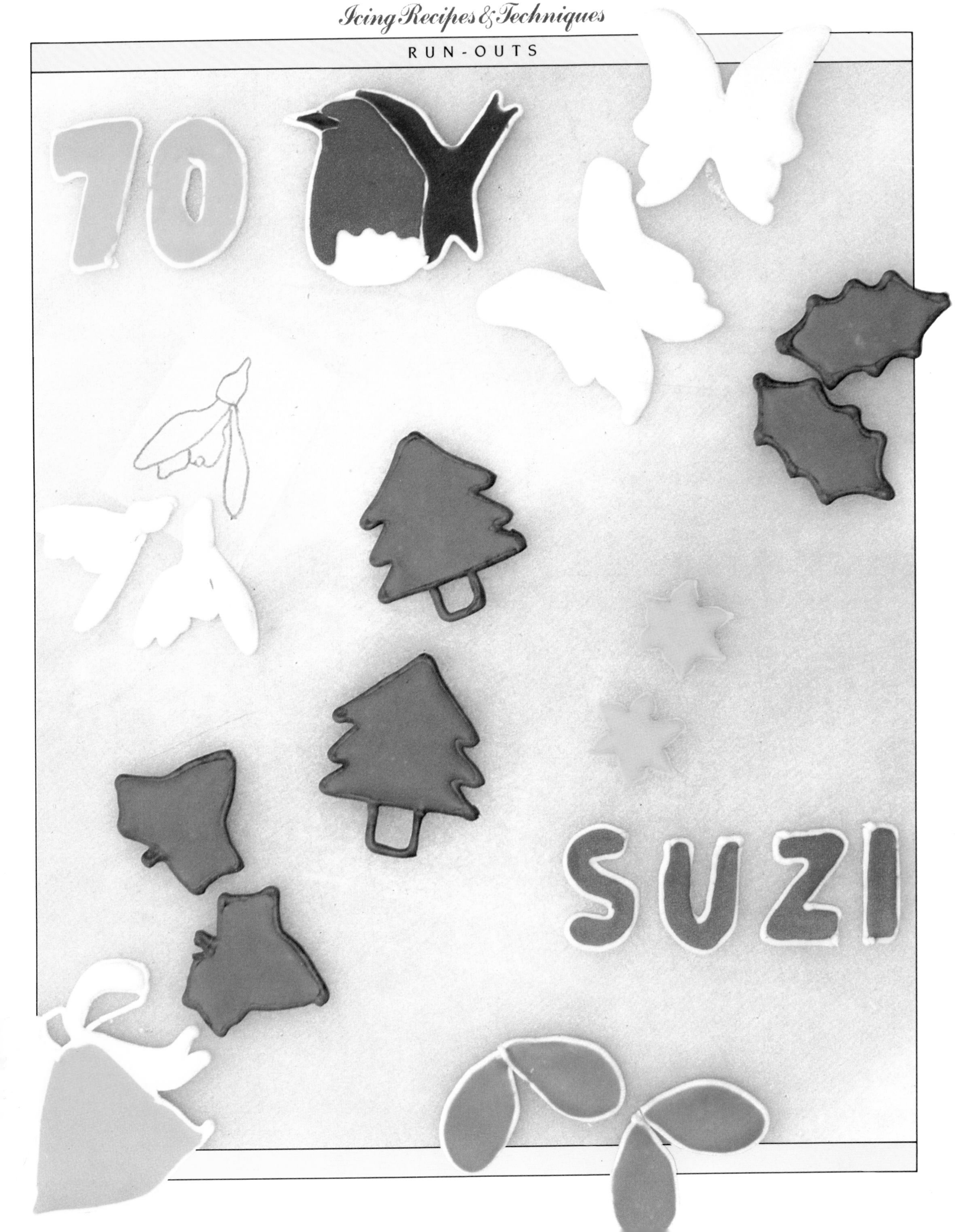
70
SUZI

This takes quite a bit of practice, but some very pretty decorations and effects can be achieved. Start with simple shapes, such as small tartlet tins, patty tins and boat-shaped moulds. Special icing moulds are available as well.

Lightly grease the mould with oil. Using a no. 2 icing nozzle, pipe trellis or lace work over the surface of the mould. Strengthen this with several lines piped around the outside edge.

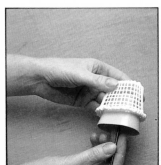

Leave for at least 24 hours to dry, then carefully remove from the mould. Store between crumpled tissue paper or cotton wool in a rigid container.

Other shapes, such as boxes, cots, can be built up by piping rectangles or squares for the sides and base on to non-stick paper. Fill these in with trellis or lace work and once dry secure the pieces together with a little icing.

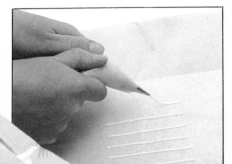 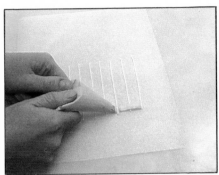 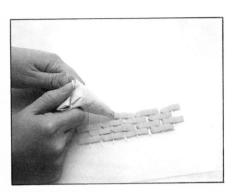

This is actually quite easy to do and gives a very professional finish to a cake. You will need two icing nozzles – a basket or ribbon nozzle and a plain nozzle (no. 2 or no. 3).

Give the cake a basic flat coat of royal icing. it does not matter if this is slightly uneven as it will be totally covered by the basket work.

With an icing bag fitted with the plain nozzle, pipe a series of vertical parallel lines around the cake at regular intervals. Leave to dry.

With a second icing bag fitted with the basket or ribbon nozzle, start the horizontal weaving at the base of the cake. Hold the nozzle at the side of one vertical line and squeeze out a ribbon of icing. Lift it over the second vertical line and finish at the side of the third vertical line. Start the next strip at the other side of the third vertical line. Repeat this all the way round the base of the cake.

Start the next row of weaving, but make sure you begin the piping at the second vertical line. Continue around the cake, building up the woven appearance.

Most designs on formally iced cakes are geometric and so must be carefully measured and worked out as any unevenness will show up dramatically in the finished cake. The best way to ensure this is to draw the design first use this drawing or design as a guide to mark out the pattern on the cake. This design is known as a template.

Ideas for designs may come from lace or other materials, wallpaper or birthday and Christmas cards. Try a simple design at first, then progress to more elaborate ones as your piping expertise improves.

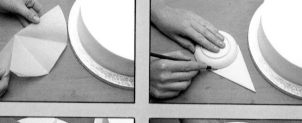

To make a template

Cut a piece of paper the exact size of the top of the cake. Fold the paper into sections, either four, six or eight. Mark a design on the top section, then cut along the line with scissors. Open out the paper to see the full effect of the design.

It is a good idea to copy the design on to some thin card. The design can then be transferred to the cake by centreing the template on the top of the cake and using a fine skewer or pin to prick or score the outline of the template. Pipe along the lines of the pattern, ensuring the icing covers the pin pricks or score marks. Any further icing which is added to build up the design can be done freehand once the basic pattern is piped.

Templates for the sides of cakes can also be made in a similar way. Measure the circumference of the cake and cut a piece of greaseproof or waxed paper exactly the same length and depth of the cake. Fold into sections to correspond with the template for the top of the cake. Draw the required design, then cut away the appropriate piece. Open out the paper to see the full design. Secure the paper in position around the cake and mark out the design with a series of pin pricks or score it with a fine skewer.

The most popular design for the side of a cake is the scallop or hanging loop. With practise you will be able to do this freehand but it is a good idea to use a template for the first attempts. You may also find it easier to tilt the cake slightly.

To pipe the loop, squeeze out a little icing and secure it in position at the start of the loop of the top edge of the cake. Squeeze out more icing so that it hangs in mid-air away from the cake. once there is a sufficient length of icing, loop it up and attach it at the end of the first scallop marking. Continue around the cake in the same way. Follow the original lines to add further icing. The icing does scrape off easily without leaving a mark, so don't worry too much about mistakes. As ever it is a good idea to practise on the side of a tin before you start the actual decorating.

I find it impossible to say which is my favourite food and equally impossible to decide upon a favourite cake. I like many different cakes for different reasons; flavour and texture are important and choosing ingredients that compliment one another takes practise. The recipes in this section include some of my particular favourites, which I hope will become your favourites too.

Favourite Cakes

SACHERTORTE

A rich, firm, yet moist chocolate cake, covered with a shiny chocolate icing. Traditionally, the only decoration it has is the name 'Sacher' written in chocolate, but I like to decorate it with whirls of fresh whipped cream and small chocolate curls.

½ cup + 2 tbsp / 150 g / 5 oz butter
⅔ cup / 150 g / 5 oz caster sugar
6 egg yolks
I tsp vanilla essence
1½ cups semisweet / 175 g / 6 oz plain chocolate, melted
I cup all-purpose / 100 g / 4 oz plain flour
¼ cup / 25 g / I oz ground almonds
2 tbsp cocoa powder
I tsp ground cinnamon
8 egg whites
Decoration:
6 tbsp apricot glaze (page 34)
I quantity mocha chocolate icing made without instant coffee (page 53)
whipped cream
chocolate curls (page 55)

Grease and base line a 23 cm / 9 in round cake tin. Mix together I tsp each flour and sugar and use to coat the sides of the tin.

Cream the butter and sugar until light and fluffy. Beat in the egg yolks one at a time. Beat in the vanilla essence.

Stir in the cooled chocolate.

Sift together the flour, ground almonds, cocoa powder and cinnamon and fold into the mixture.

Whisk the egg whites until stiff and fold into the chocolate mixture.

Transfer the mixture to the prepared tin. Level the surface and bake at 190°C / 375°F / Gas 5 for about 55 minutes until risen and firm to the touch. Leave to cool. Transfer to a wire rack and leave until cold.

Split the cake horizontally and spread with half the apricot glaze. Sandwich together and brush the remaining glaze over the top and sides of the cake.

Beat the mocha chocolate icing until smooth, then pour over the cake, smoothing the sides with a palette knife.

Leave until the icing is completely set, then decorate with whipped cream and chocolate curls.

CARROT CAKE

This is a deliciously moist cake made with finely grated carrot and lots of ground or finely chopped nuts. The strong, sweet flavour of passion fruit complements it particularly well.

7 eggs, separated
1 cup / 200 g / 7 oz caster sugar
¾ cup / 125 g / 4 oz ground almonds
¾ cup / 125 g / 4 oz shelled walnuts or toasted hazelnuts, ground or very finely chopped
⅓ cup shredded / 50 g / 2 oz desiccated coconut
3 cups / 300 g / 10 oz carrots, peeled and finely grated
½ cup / 50 g / 2 oz self-raising flour, sifted
grated rind of 1 lemon or orange
Icing and decoration:
4 passion fruit
1½ quantity crème au beurre (page 42)
1 tsp lemon or orange juice
6 tbsp / 75 g / 3 oz almond paste (page 66)
orange food colouring
12 small pieces angelica

Grease and base line a 25 cm / 10 in round cake tin.

Whisk the egg yolks with half the sugar until pale and thick. Stir in the ground almonds, walnuts, coconut, carrots, flour and lemon rind.

Whisk the egg whites until stiff, then whisk in the remaining sugar a little at a time until the mixture is really thick.

Fold the carrot mixture into the egg whites carefully.

Transfer the mixture to the prepared tin, level the surface and bake at 180°C / 350°F / Gas 4 for about 45 minutes until risen and firm to the touch.

Leave to cool in the tin, then transfer to a wire rack. Invert the cake tin over the cake and leave until completely cold.

Split the passion fruit and put the pulp into a nylon sieve over a small bowl. Press out the juice with a wooden spoon.

Mix together the crème au beurre, passion fruit juice and lemon juice until smooth.

Split the cake in half horizontally and sandwich together with a generous quarter of the icing. Use the remaining icing to swirl over the top and sides of the cake. Mark the cake into 12 portions.

Colour the almond paste with food colouring and shape into 12 carrots. Mark lines across each one with a knife. Stick pieces of angelica into each carrot top and arrange the carrots round the top edge of the cake.

This is no-cook cake which takes minutes to prepare and keeps your guests guessing for ages! It's an ideal way to use up the off-cuts from rich fruit cakes.

I lb / 450 g / I lb leftover rich fruit cake
¼–½ cup / 50–75 g / 2–3 oz apricot jam or marmalade
2 tbsp rum or other spirit, or fruit juice
I cup semisweet / 100 g / 4 oz plain chocolate, melted
¼ cup / 25 g / I oz white or milk chocolate, melted

Crumble the fruit cake in a bowl, or process in a food processor.

Add the jam, depending on how moist the cake is, and the rum and mix well.

On a piece of non-stick paper or cling film, shape the mixture into a long, triangular shape. The cake may be stored in the refrigerator for weeks like this.

Place the cake on a wire rack over a baking sheet or tray, and spread the sides and ends with the plain chocolate.

Fill a small paper piping bag with the white or milk chocolate. Snip off the end and drizzle the chocolate over the cake decoratively. Chill until firm, then transfer to a serving plate. Serve, cut in thin slices.

This isn't really a gâteau, but it is so quick to make and delicious to eat. It uses broken biscuits to form the main part of the 'cake'.

½ lb plain sweet cookies / 225 g / 8 oz plain sweet biscuits
½ cup / 100 g / 4 oz butter
I egg, beaten
generous ½ cup / 150 g / 5 oz soft light brown sugar
½ cup / 50 g / 2 oz shelled walnuts, chopped
I tsp vanilla essence
½ quantity of butter cream or crème au beurre in a plain, coffee or orange flavour (page 42)
walnut halves

Break the biscuits into small pieces in a bowl.

Melt the butter, then add the egg and sugar and bring slowly to the boil, stirring all the time. Boil for I minute.

Pour over the biscuits, then add the chopped walnuts and vanilla essence. Mix well until the biscuit pieces are evenly coated.

Press the mixture into an 18 cm / 7 in greased sandwich tin and chill until firm.

Turn the cake out onto a plate and spread with butter cream. Pipe a decorative border, if wished. Decorate with walnut halves.

RASPBERRY AND HAZELNUT GATEAU

The combination of raspberries with hazelnuts is a particularly good one. The cake may be made in advance, but do not fill it until the day it is required as the juice from the raspberries will be inclined to seep into the cake layers.

6 eggs, separated
I tsp vanilla essence
1 cup / 225 g / 8 oz caster sugar
¾ cup / 225 g / 8 oz toasted hazelnuts, ground
6 tbsp dry white breadcrumbs
I tsp baking powder
pinch salt
Filling and decoration:
2 cups / 450 g / I lb fresh raspberries
2 cups whipping / 450 ml / ¾ pt double cream
½ quantity redcurrant glaze (page 34)
tiny leaves or mint sprigs

Grease and base line three 20 cm / 8 in sandwich tins with non-stick paper.

Whisk the egg yolks with the vanilla essence and half the sugar until pale and thick. Stir in the hazelnuts, breadcrumbs and baking powder.

Whisk the egg whites with a pinch of salt until stiff. Add the remaining sugar a little at a time, whisking well between each addition.

Fold the nut mixture into the egg white mixture until evenly combined. Transfer to the prepared tins and level the surface of each.

Bake at 190°C / 375°F / Gas 5 for 25–30 minutes until risen and firm to the touch. Cool slightly in the tins, then transfer to a wire rack and invert the cake tins over the cakes. Leave until completely cold.

Wash and pick over the raspberries.

Whip the cream until it just holds its shape. Reserve a little to pipe, then use a very scant half to sandwich the layers using half the raspberries as well. Arrange the remaining raspberries on the top layer of sponge and brush carefully with the redcurrant glaze. Chill until set.

Spread the remaining cream over the sides of the cake. Pipe swirls on top of the cake and decorate with the tiny leaves.

COFFEE GALETTE

Thin layers of sponge cake may be sandwiched together with many different fillings to make a variety of delicious gâteaux; the side coating and decorations can be varied to suit the desired flavour. This recipe for a coffee-flavoured cake can be transformed into almost any flavour to give you an amazingly wide choice. Try lemon, orange, chocolate with praline, to name but a few!

4-egg quantity whisked sponge baked in 6 × 20 cm / 8 in rounds (page 25)

---

1 quantity coffee marshmallow butter cream 2 (page 44)

½ quantity coffee glacé icing (page 40)

½ cup / 50 g / 2 oz nibbed almonds, toasted, or chocolate, grated chocolate coffee beans

---

Sandwich the sponge layers together using about half of the butter cream.

Spread the glacé icing over the top layer of sponge and leave until set firm.

Use most of the remaining butter cream to cover the sides of the cake. Carefully press the grated chocolate or nuts onto the sides of the cake to evenly coat it.

Use remaining butter cream to pipe rosettes around the top edge of the cake. Decorate with chocolate coffee beans.

CONCORDE CAKE

Although it is not really a cake in the traditional sense, Concorde is a delightful mixture of meringue, chocolate mousse and whipped cream!

4 egg whites
1 cup / 225 g / 8 oz caster sugar
Mousse filling:
1½ cups semisweet / 175 g / 6 oz plain chocolate
2 egg yolks
½ cup / 100 ml / 4 fl oz water
½ cup whipping / 100 ml / 4 fl oz double cream
4 egg whites
1½ tbsp / 40 g / 1½ oz caster sugar
Decoration:
⅔ cup whipping / 150 ml / ¼ pt double cream
small chocolate decorations (page 57)

Draw two 20 cm / 8 in circles on non-stick paper. Place on baking sheets.

Whisk the egg whites with a pinch of salt until stiff. Whisk in the sugar a little at a time until the meringue mixture is really thick and white.

Spoon the mixture into a piping bag fitted with a large star nozzle. Pipe 16 tiny rosettes. Use the remaining meringue to make the meringue nests. Starting at the centre of each paper circle, pipe in continuous circles to cover the paper. Pipe one or two circles on the outside edge of each round to complete the nests.

Bake at 130°C / 250°F / Gas ½ for 2 hours. Remove the tiny rosettes after 1 hour. Leave the meringue until cold.

For the filling, melt the chocolate in a bowl over hot water. Remove from the heat, stir in the egg yolks, then slowly beat in the water.

Whip the cream until it just holds its shape, then fold into the chocolate mixture.

Whisk the egg whites until stiff, then add the sugar a little at a time, whisking well between each addition. Fold the egg white mixture into the chocolate. Spoon into the meringue nests and chill for several hours until firm.

For the decoration, whip the cream and place in a piping bag fitted with a star nozzle.

Place the meringue nests, one on top of the other. Pipe cream between the two layers, then sandwich the tiny rosettes together in pairs.

Pipe any remaining cream on the top of the cake and decorate with the rosette pairs and chocolate decorations.

A Swiss roll covered with brightly coloured almond paste makes this cake a pretty centrepiece for the Christmas teatable.

I Swiss (jelly) roll filled with 6 tbsp jam or ½ quantity butter cream (pages 24 and 42)
½ quantity almond paste (page 66)
red and green edible food colourings
3–4 tbsp apricot glaze (page 34)

Colour three-quarters of the almond paste with red colouring. Reserve a tiny amount of natural almond paste, then colour the remaining paste with green colouring.

Measure the length and circumference of the Swiss (jelly) roll with two pieces of string.

Roll out the red paste on a surface lightly sprinkled with icing sugar, to a rectangle 2.5 cm / 1 in larger than the length and circumference of the cake. Trim the edges neatly.

Cut 1 cm / ½ in slashes along both short edges of the paste, at regular intervals. Use most of the trimmings to make 2 rounds large enough to cover the ends of the roll. Brush with apricot glaze and press in place.

Brush the red paste with apricot glaze and carefully roll it round the roll to cover it completely. Squeeze the cake at both ends about 4 cm / 1½ in from each end to make a more realistic cracker.

Roll out the green paste to make two ribbons and trim to size. Arrange these around the cake on the 'squeezed' sections and secure with apricot glaze.

Use any green almond paste trimmings to make holly and mistletoe leaves, and red and natural paste for holly and mistletoe berries. Arrange a garland in the centre of the cracker and secure with apricot glaze.

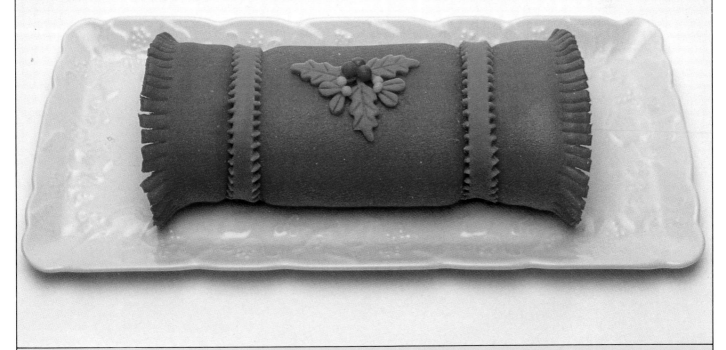

APRICOT AND ALMOND GATEAU

I'm very fond of almond paste and this combination of apricots with almonds is a classic one, particularly in French pastries.

3-egg quantity Genoese sponge mixture (page 25)
2 × 425 g / 15 oz cans apricot halves, drained
1¼ cups whipping / 300 ml / ½ pt double cream
I quantity apricot glaze (page 34)
¾ cup / 175 g / 6 oz almond paste (page 66)
a few flaked almonds, toasted

Grease and base line three 20 cm / 8 in sandwich tins and divide the sponge mixture between the prepared tins. Bake at 190°C / 375°F / Gas 5 for 10–15 minutes, until risen and firm to the touch. Remove from the tins and cool on a wire rack.

Use sufficient apricot halves to completely cover one layer of sponge. Chop the remaining apricots.

Whip the cream and reserve one-third in a piping bag fitted with a large star nozzle. Fold the chopped apricots into the remaining two-thirds and use to sandwich the cakes together finishing with the layer covered with the apricot halves.

Brush the sides of the cake with apricot glaze.

On a surface lightly sifted with icing sugar, roll out the almond paste to a strip of the exact size to cover the sides of the cake. Trim and press gently into position.

Sprinkle the apricot halves with the flaked almonds, then brush with apricot glaze. Decorate with rosettes of the reserved whipped cream and chill until required.

FRUIT-TOPPED RICH CHEESECAKE

This cheesecake is one of my favourites. Serve it just as it is or decorate with whatever fruit is in season.

Base:

2½–3 cups graham crackers / 200 g / 7 oz digestive biscuits, crushed
7 tbsp / 100 g / 3½ oz butter, melted

Filling:

5 cups cream / 900 g / 2 lb cream or curd cheese
1 cup / 225 g / 8 oz caster sugar
3 tbsp all-purpose / 40 g / 1½ oz plain flour
5 eggs
⅔ cup whipping / 150 ml / ¼ pt double cream
grated rind 1 large lemon

Topping:

selection of fresh fruits in season: about 225 g / ½ lb
lemon juice
½ quantity apricot glaze (page 34)

Mix together the digestive biscuits and butter and press on to the base of a 24 cm / 9½ in spring-release tin. Chill.

Mix together all the ingredients for the filling until evenly combined. Pour over the base and bake at 230°C / 450°F / Gas 8 for 15 minutes. Reduce the temperature to 110°C / 225°F / Gas ¼ for a further 1 hour. Turn off the heat and leave the cake to cool in the oven. When completely cold, remove from the tin. Prepare the fruits according to type and dip any that will discolour in lemon juice. Arrange attractively over the surface of the cake. Brush with apricot glaze and serve as soon as possible after decorating.

*This charming novelty cake is simply to make and will delight any small child
on a birthday or other occasion.*

2 × 20 cm / 8 in Victoria layer / 2 × 20 cm / 8 in Victoria sandwich cakes (page 22)
1 quantity butter cream (page 42)
pink and brown edible food colouring
1½ cups shredded / 100 g / 4 oz desiccated coconut
1 glacé cherry
approx. 45 cm / 18 in ribbon

Cut a 13 cm / 5½ in square from the centre of one cake. Cut a 13 cm / 5½ in circle from the second cake. Cut 4 small sections from the remaining circle.

Reserve 2 tbsp butter cream and colour it with brown food colouring or coffee essence. Colour remaining butter cream pale pink.

Sandwich together sections 1 and 2, and 3 and 4 with a little pink butter cream, for the ears. Cover ears with a thin layer of pink butter cream.

Cover the round and square sections with pink butter cream and the small sections 5, 6, 7 and 8.

Arrange all the sections in position on a large plate or tray as shown in diagram 2.

Gently press the desiccated coconut all over the surface of the cake until evenly coated.

Using a piping bag filled with brown butter cream and fitted with a no. 2 writing nozzle, pipe the face and paw markings. Press in position ½ glacé cherry for the nose and two quarters for the eyes.

Tie the ribbon in a bow and arrange in position. If wished candleholders with birthday candles may be used as buttons down the front of the bunny.

STRAWBERRY LAYER CAKE

The halved strawberries around the sides of this cake give a decorative finish, and adding the liqueur makes all the difference to the flavour.

3-egg quantity Genoese sponge mixture baked in two 20 cm / 8 in sandwich tins (layer cake pans) (page 25)
3 cups / 450 g / 1 lb medium-sized strawberries
¼ cup confectioners' / 50 g / 2 oz icing sugar, plus extra for dredging
1⅓ cups / 225 g / 8 oz cream or curd cheese
1 tbsp gelatin / 15 g / ½ oz gelatine
2 tbsp water
2 tbsp fraise, kirsch or other liqueur
1¼ cups whipping / 300 ml / ½ pt double cream

Line the sides of an 18 cm / 7 in round cake tin with non-stick paper. Press one sponge cake into the base of the tin, trimming if necessary.

Choose about 10 even-sized strawberries. Hull them and cut each one in half. Press strawberries, cut side out, against the side of the tin, around the outside edge of the cake.

Hull 175 g / 6 oz strawberries and purée with the icing sugar and cream cheese until smooth. Dissolve the gelatine in the water over a gentle heat and stir into the strawberry mixture with the fraise.

Whip half the cream until it holds its shape, then fold into the strawberry mixture. Carefully pour the strawberry mixture into the tin without dislodging the strawberry halves.

Chill until lightly set, then place the second sponge layer on top, trimming if necessary. Chill for several hours until firm.

Carefully remove cake from the tin. Peel away the non-stick paper.

Whip the remaining cream until it just holds its shape. Spoon into a piping bag fitted with a star nozzle. Sprinkle the top of the cake with icing sugar, then decorate with piped cream and remaining strawberries. Serve at once.

LEMON CREAM HEART

A light whisked sponge, split, filled and covered with a delicious lemon cream, makes an ideal cake for a special celebration tea. If you don't own a heart-shaped tin, simply make a round one in two 20 cm / 8 in sandwich tins and follow the chart on page 25 for cooking instructions.

3-egg quantity whisked sponge mixture (page 24)
Filling:
6 tbsp / 75 g / 3 oz butter
½ cup / 100 g / 4 oz granulated sugar
2 eggs, beaten
grated rind and juice of 2 small lemons or 1 very large lemon
⅔ cup whipping / 150 ml / ¼ pt double cream
Decoration:
fresh yellow flowers and sprigs of fern

Grease and flour a 1.5 l / 2½ pt heart-shaped cake tin.

Pour the sponge mixture into the tin and bake at 190°C / 375°F / Gas 5 for about 20 minutes until risen and firm to the touch. Allow to cool in the tin, then transfer to a wire rack and invert the tin over the cake. Leave until cold.

Melt the butter in a bowl over a saucepan of simmering water. Stir in the sugar, eggs, lemon rind and juice and stir well. Cook for about 20–25 minutes, stirring frequently, until the mixture is thick. Chill well.

Whip the cream, then fold in the lemon mixture.

Split the cake and sandwich together with about one-quarter of the lemon cream. Use the remaining cream to cover the surface of the cake, swirling it decoratively. Decorate with flowers and fern sprigs.

OLD-FASHIONED ALMOND CAKE

The combination of ground almonds and ground rice makes this cake wonderfully moist. It can be stored for weeks, if it lasts that long, and seems to improve in flavour. It is not essential to decorate it, but if you do, add the decorations on the day of serving.

1 cup / 225 g / 8 oz butter, softened
1 cup / 225 g / 8 oz caster sugar
3 eggs, beaten
½ tsp almond essence
1 cup / 100 g / 4 oz ground almonds
1 cup / 100 g / 4 oz ground rice
½ cup / 50 g / 2 oz self-raising flour, sifted
Decoration:
1 tbsp apricot glaze (page 34)
3 tbsp slivered / 3 tbsp flaked almonds, toasted
a little glacé icing (page 40)

Grease and base-line a 20 cm / 8 in round cake tin.

Cream the butter and sugar until light and fluffy. Beat in the eggs, a little at a time, then beat in the almond essence.

Mix together the ground almonds, ground rice and flour and fold into the creamed mixture.

Transfer the mixture to the prepared tin. Bake at 170°C / 325°F / Gas 3 for 1¼–1½ hours until risen and firm to the touch. Cool in the tin, then turn out on to a wire rack. Invert the tin over the cake and leave until cold.

Brush the top of the cake with apricot glaze, sprinkle with almonds, then drizzle with a little glacé icing.

I've combined a favourite mixture of bananas and cream with toasted coconut and maraschino cherries to make this tropically flavoured cake. For total authenticity try adding a dash of white rum to the fresh cream!

3 large ripe bananas, peeled

½ cup / 100 g / 4 oz butter, softened

½ cup + 2 tbsp / 150 g / 5 oz soft brown sugar

2 eggs, beaten

2 cups all-purpose / 225 g / 8 oz plain flour

1 tbsp baking powder

Decoration:

1¼ cups whipping / 300 ml / ½ pt double cream

⅔ cup shredded / 50 g / 2 oz desiccated coconut, toasted

banana slices, dipped in lemon juice

maraschino cherries

Grease and base line a 20 cm / 8 in round cake tin.

Mash the bananas well. Beat the butter and sugar until light and fluffy, then beat in the eggs until well mixed. Fold in the bananas.

Sift the flour and baking powder together and fold into the mixture.

Transfer the mixture to the prepared tin. Level the surface, then make a slight dip in the centre Bake at 180°C / 350°F / Gas 4 for about 1 hour until a skewer placed in the centre of the cake comes out clean. Cool on a wire rack, covered by the inverted tin. When cold, split the cake horizontally into three.

Whip the cream until it stands in soft peaks and use about three-quarters to fill and cover the whole surface of the cake. Press coconut all over the cream. Use the remaining cream to pipe decorative swirls over the top of the cake and decorate with banana slices and cherries. Serve on the day of decorating.

MURRUMBIDGEE CAKE

This is an incredibly rich fruit and nut cake that originated in Australia. It really needs no decoration whatsoever as the slices are so attractive.

1½ cups / 175 g / 6 oz whole brazil nuts, shelled
1½ cups / 175 g / 6 oz walnuts, shelled
1½ cups / 225 g / 8 oz stoned dates
1 cup / 100 g / 4 oz mixed candied peel, chopped
¼ cup / 50 g / 2 oz *each* red, green and yellow glacé cherries
⅓ cup / 50 g / 2 oz raisins
¾ cup all-purpose / 75 g / 3 oz plain flour
pinch salt
½ tsp baking powder
½ cup / 100 g / 4 oz soft, light brown sugar
3 eggs, beaten
1 tsp vanilla essence
rum or other spirit, as wished
2 tbsp apricot glaze (page 34)

Grease and line an 18 cm / 7 in round cake tin.

Mix all the fruits and nuts together.

Sift the flour, salt and baking powder into a bowl. Stir in the sugar.

Add the fruit to the dry ingredients and toss well to evenly coat with the flour.

Add the beaten eggs and vanilla essence and mix well.

Transfer the mixture to the prepared tin, and press the mixture down with the back of a spoon.

Bake at 150°C / 300°F / Gas 2 for 1½–1¾ hours until firm and golden. A skewer should come out of the cake cleanly if the cake is cooked. Cover with foil if overbrowning on the surface occurs during cooking time.

Cool in the tin, then spoon over 2 tbsp rum or other spirit. Leave to go cold, then wrap in cling film and foil, and store in a cool dry place.

Leave the cake to mature for at least one month, adding more rum as required.

Before serving, brush cake with apricot glaze.

DEVIL'S FOOD CAKE

This is a very dark chocolate cake with a very light spongy texture. It is coated in chocolate fudge icing, so for contrast I like to fill it with whipped fresh cream.

I cup / 225 ml / 8 fl oz milk
I tbsp lemon juice or vinegar
2¼ cups all-purpose / 225 g / 8 oz plain flour
I tsp baking / I tsp bicarbonate of soda
¼ cup / 50 g / 2 oz cocoa powder
½ cup / 100 g / 4 oz butter or margarine
I cup / 225 g / 8 oz soft brown sugar
2 eggs, beaten
⅔ cup whipping / 150 ml / ¼ pt double cream
I½ quantity chocolate fudge icing (page 48)

Grease and base line two 23 cm / 9 in sandwich tins.

Mix the milk with the lemon juice and put to one side.

Sift the flour, bicarbonate of soda and cocoa powder into a bowl.

Cream the butter and sugar together until light and fluffy, then slowly beat in the eggs a little at a time.

Fold in the dry ingredients alternately with the soured milk.

Spoon the mixture into the prepared tins, level the surface and bake at 180°C / 350°F / Gas 4 for about 25 minutes until risen and firm to the touch.

Leave to cool in the tin, then transfer to a wire rack and leave until completely cold. Whip the cream until stiff and use to sandwich the cake layers together.

Place the cake on a plate and spread the fudge icing over the top and sides to cover it completely.

This is an unusual fruit cake made with crystallized pineapple, ginger, glacé cherries and almonds as well as sultanas. Lighter than the rich fruit cake recipe given on page 26, this cake is ideal for a birthday cake or everyday eating. It actually takes about 1½ quantities of easy fondant icing to cover the cake, so any trimmings can be used in a variety of ways to give different finishes, suitable for different occasions.
I couldn't resist using these adorable marzipan animals!

1 cup / 225 g / 8 oz butter, softened
1 cup / 225 g / 8 oz caster sugar
4 eggs, beaten
2 tbsp light corn syrup / 2 tbsp golden syrup
grated rind of 1 orange and 1 lemon
2½ cups all-purpose / 300 g / 10 oz plain flour
2 cups seedless white raisins / 350 g / 12 oz sultanas
½ cup candied / 100 g / 4 oz crystallized pineapple, chopped
½ cup candied / 100 g / 4 oz crystallized ginger, chopped
¾ cup candied / 100 g / 4 oz glacé cherries, halved
¾ cup / 100 g / 4 oz blanched almonds, roughly chopped
Decoration:
6 tbsp apricot glaze (page 34)
double quantity easy fondant icing (page 59)
⅔ cup / 50 g / 2 oz long thread or desiccated (shredded) coconut
black and green edible food colourings
selection of almond paste animals (page 00)

Grease and line a 23 cm / 9 in round cake tin.

Cream together the butter and sugar until light and fluffy. Beat in the eggs, a little at a time, then beat in the golden syrup, orange and lemon rinds.

Sift the flour, stir in the fruits and nuts and fold into the creamed mixture until evenly mixed. Add a little milk, if necessary, to give a dropping consistency.

Transfer the mixture to the prepared tin. Level the surface, then make a slight dip in the centre. Bake at 150°C / 300°F / Gas 2 for 2–2¼ hours until a skewer inserted in the centre of the cake comes out clean.

Leave to cool in the tin, then transfer to a wire rack. Invert the tin over the cake and leave to go cold.

Brush the cake all over with apricot glaze, then roll out the fondant icing on a surface lightly sprinkled with icing sugar. Use to cover the cake (see page 00 for method). Neaten the edges and reserve the trimmings.

Colour about one-quarter of the reserved fondant with black colouring (spare fondant can be kept for later use) and roll into short lengths to make the bars of the cage, attaching each one as you roll it.

Rub the coconut with a few drops of green colouring, in a small bowl, until evenly coloured. Sprinkle over the centre of the cake and top with the almond paste animals.

Trace-off templates

The shapes shown on the following pages are ready to trace-off for run-out designs. Use greaseproof or waxed paper and trace round the individual outlines with a thick pencil. Use as described on pages 98–99.

ABCDEFGHIJKLM

NOPQRSTUVWXYZ

1 2 3 4 5 6

7 8 9 10

A note on measures

The recipes in this book give quantities in metric, imperial and American measures. The metric measures are based on the standard 25 g = 1 oz and 600 ml = 1 pint units. The American measures are based on the standard 8 oz cup measure (solids and liquids).

Spoon measures are level unless otherwise stated and are based on the British Standard teaspoon and tablespoon. If you have a set of metric measuring spoons, the equivalents are 5 ml = 1 teaspoon and 15 ml = 1 tablespoon.

Each set of measures in the recipes has been calculated separately, so remember to follow only one set as the measures are not interchangeable.

British/American terms

The list below gives some American equivalents or substitutes for the terms and ingredients used in this book.

Ingredients

British	American
almonds, flaked	almonds, slivered
bicarbonate of soda	baking soda
bilberries	blueberries
biscuits	cookies
cocktail stick	toothpick
coconut, desiccated	coconut, shredded
cornflour	cornstarch
crystallized fruit	candied fruit
chocolate caraque	chocolate curls
chocolate, plain	chocolate, semi-sweet
cream, double	cream, heavy, or use whipping cream
cream, single	cream, light
cream, sour	cream, dairy sour cream
digestive biscuit crumbs	graham cracker crumbs
essence	extract
flour, plain	flour, all-purpose
flour, self-raising	flour, self-raising
glacé cherries	candied cherries
golden syrup	light corn syrup
nutmeg, grated	nutmeg, ground
sugar, caster	sugar, superfine
sugar, demerara	sugar, light brown granulated
sugar, icing	sugar, confectioners'
sultanas	golden raisins, or seedless white raisins
top of milk	half-and-half
treacle	molasses

Equipment and terms

aluminium foil	aluminium foil
baking sheet	cookie sheet
biscuit cutters	cookie cutters
cake tin	cake pan

NOTES

Useful addresses

UK

The following specialist shops have a mail order service and will supply catalogues on request. Some also have showrooms; enquire about times of opening so that you can pay them a visit.

Guy Paul and Co. Ltd

Unit B4, A1 Industrial Park, Little End Road, Eaton Socon, Cambs PE19 3JH

Cookcraft Club Ltd

20 Canterbury Road, Herne Bay, Kent CT6 5DJ

Mary Ford Cake Artistry Centre

28–30 Southbourne Grove, Southbourne, Bournemouth, Dorset BH6 3RA

Baker Smith Ltd

65 The Street, Tongham, Farnham, Surrey GU10 1DD

Elizabeth David Ltd

46 Bourne Street, London SW1W 8JD

David Mellor

4 Sloane Square, London SW1W 8EE

USA

Wilton Enterprises Inc

2240 West 75th Street, Woodridge, Illinois 60517
The main manufacturer of cake decorating equipment

H. Roth & Son Paprika Co

1577 First Avenue, New York, NY 10028

Paprika's Weiss

1546 2nd Avenue, New York, NY 10021

Bridge Co

214 East 52nd Street, New York, NY 10022

The three suppliers listed above, all in New York City, run a mail order service; apply for catalogues

Acknowledgements

I would like to thank Guy Paul and Co Ltd, of Eaton Socon, Cambridgeshire, for kindly supplying some of the items for photography.

I would also like to thank my family for their help and encouragement throughout the testing of recipes and, in particular, thanks to Anne, Suzi and Alison for their help behind the scenes during the photographic sessions.